I0050417

Published by Marios Mamzeris

ISBN: 978-1-0687102-4-7

First Edition

Disclaimer

This book, "Crypto Investment Essentials: A Practical Handbook for Beginner to Intermediate Investors" by Marios Mamzeris, is for educational and informational purposes only. It should not be considered as financial, investment, legal, or trading advice. The content of this guide is based on the author's research and experience and is provided "as is," without any guarantees, express or implied.

The author and publisher do not guarantee the accuracy, completeness, or timeliness of the information. Readers are strongly encouraged to conduct their own research and consult with qualified financial professionals before making any investment decisions.

Investing in cryptocurrencies and digital assets carries inherent risks, including market volatility, regulatory changes, and potential capital loss. The strategies, considerations, and insights shared in this book are subject to change and may not be suitable for all individuals. Individual results may vary, and past performance is not indicative of future results.

Table of Contents

Abstract

Investing in cryptocurrencies presents a unique blend of opportunities and risks, offering a potentially rewarding journey for investors. A strategic and well-informed approach is essential to successfully navigating this volatile market. The comprehensive guide, "Crypto Investment Essentials: A Practical Handbook for Beginner to Intermediate Investors," provides a robust framework to help both novice and experienced investors make informed decisions aligned with their financial objectives and risk tolerance, paving the way for potential financial success.

This guide explores the core concepts of cryptocurrencies and blockchain technology, enabling investors to look beyond market hype and evaluate the inherent value and potential of various digital assets. It then leads investors through the process of setting investment goals, managing portfolios, and diversifying their holdings to minimise risks.

Investors will uncover advanced trading strategies, including technical and fundamental analysis techniques, as well as insights into the environmental impact of cryptocurrency mining and the emerging opportunities in staking and yield farming. The book also examines the advantages and considerations of investing in cryptocurrency ETFs and emphasises the importance of effective risk management.

Acknowledging the importance of security and regulatory compliance, this guide offers detailed advice on selecting reputable exchanges, managing personal wallets, and navigating the evolving regulatory landscape. It also provides practical tax planning strategies to help investors optimise their returns.

By combining technical expertise, real-world case studies, and a comprehensive investment approach, this book empowers investors to make well-informed decisions, cultivate disciplined trading habits, and navigate the dynamic cryptocurrency market with confidence. Whether one is an experienced investor or new to the crypto space, this all-encompassing guide is an indispensable resource for achieving long-term success in cryptocurrency investing.

Preface

Dear Readers,

Welcome to "Crypto Investment Essentials: A Practical Handbook for Beginner to Intermediate Investors." This book has been a labour of love, born out of a decade-long journey in the realms of cryptocurrencies, coupled with my experience in trading stocks and foreign exchange. Over the years, friends and colleagues have approached me seeking guidance on navigating the complex world of crypto investments. Their curiosity and eagerness to learn inspired me to distil my knowledge and experiences into this comprehensive guide.

Reflecting on my own crypto journey, I can't help but chuckle at the memory of paying for my Master's in Cryptocurrencies and Blockchain with Bitcoin back in 2017, when it was priced at around $1,800 per Bitcoin. In hindsight, that decision may have made it one of the most expensive degrees in today's terms. However, every experience, even the costly ones, has contributed to shaping my understanding of the crypto landscape.

As you delve into the pages of this book, I urge you to approach your investment decisions with caution and diligence. Remember the importance of portfolio management and diversification, as highlighted in the chapters on setting investment goals. Think twice before making significant moves, and always adhere to your established rules and strategies.

My wife and daughter have been my pillars of support and inspiration in crafting this handbook. Their encouragement and positive feedback from close friends and esteemed colleagues motivated me to share my insights and expertise with a broader audience.

My goal for this book is not just to inform but to inspire and empower. I want to equip you with the knowledge and tools to make informed decisions, cultivate disciplined trading habits, and navigate the dynamic cryptocurrency market with confidence. The strategies outlined in this book are designed to empower you, the reader, to take control of your investment journey and apply them wisely.

As you embark on this educational voyage through the world of cryptocurrency investing, remember to tread carefully, stay informed, and always align your actions with your financial goals and risk tolerance. This focus and clear-minded approach will guide you through the complexities of the cryptocurrency market.

I wish you success and prosperity in your crypto investment endeavours.

Warm regards,
Marios Mamzeris

Investing in Cryptocurrencies

Cryptocurrency investment, with its potential for significant returns, is a field of both opportunities and risks. The market's high volatility, rapid technological advancements, and evolving regulatory landscape necessitate a strategic and well-informed approach. This is crucial for managing risks and maximising returns in this dynamic environment, offering a promising future for investors.

To succeed in this dynamic environment, investors need a deep understanding of blockchain technology, different types of digital assets, and the fundamental drivers of cryptocurrency markets. The "Crypto Investment Essentials" is a comprehensive guide, leaving no stone unturned, designed to provide novice and experienced investors with the knowledge and tools to make well-informed decisions based on their financial goals and risk tolerance.

The guide starts by exploring the core concepts of cryptocurrencies and blockchain technology. This helps readers see beyond market hype and evaluate the value and potential of different digital assets. It then covers setting investment goals, managing portfolios, and diversifying holdings to mitigate risks, ensuring a secure and protected investment journey.

As the guide progresses, investors will learn advanced trading strategies, including technical and fundamental analysis techniques. They will also learn about the environmental impact of cryptocurrency mining and the emerging opportunities in staking and yield farming. The guide also examines the advantages and considerations of investing in cryptocurrency exchange-traded funds (ETFs) and emphasises effective risk management.

Recognising the significance of security and regulatory compliance is paramount in cryptocurrency investment. This guide offers detailed advice on selecting reputable exchanges, managing personal wallets, and navigating the evolving regulatory landscape. Additionally, it provides practical tax planning strategies to help investors protect their assets and optimise their returns.

By combining technical expertise, real-world case studies, and a comprehensive investment approach, this guide empowers investors to make well-informed decisions, cultivate disciplined trading habits, and navigate the dynamic cryptocurrency market with confidence. Whether the reader is an experienced investor or new to the crypto space, this all-encompassing guide is indispensable for achieving long-term success in cryptocurrency investing.

Chapter 1

Understanding the Basics

It is essential to have a basic understanding of cryptocurrencies and blockchain technology before making any investment decisions. It is crucial to differentiate between coins and tokens, comprehend blockchain mechanics, and understand the importance of decentralisation in cryptocurrencies.

This knowledge will enable investors to look beyond market hype and make informed decisions based on different cryptocurrencies' technological potential and usefulness.

The Technology Behind Cryptocurrencies: A Deeper Dive

For readers seeking to explore the technical foundations of cryptocurrencies, this chapter provides an overview of the key concepts that underpin this revolutionary technology. Though not essential for guiding investment decisions, grasping these technical aspects can enhance one's ability to evaluate the potential and risks associated with various cryptocurrencies.

How Blockchain Works (Using Bitcoin as an Example)

At the core of cryptocurrencies like Bitcoin lies a revolutionary system known as a blockchain. Imagine a never-ending chain made up of individual data blocks, each holding a collection of transactions. This setup is similar to storing information in traditional databases or logbooks.

However, what sets blockchain apart is its decentralised nature. Instead of storing data on a central server like in a traditional system, the information on a blockchain is distributed and shared equally among all participants. This means that every participant in the blockchain network has an identical copy of the ledger, ensuring transparency and security across the board.

When a transaction occurs on the Bitcoin network, it is bundled into a block along with other recent transactions. This block is then added to the end of the blockchain through a process called mining. Mining is the process of validating and adding new transactions to the blockchain. Miners use powerful computers to solve complex mathematical problems, and the first miner to solve the problem has their block added to the chain. This process is crucial for maintaining the security and integrity of the blockchain.

Once a block is added, it becomes an immutable part of the blockchain's history. This is because each block contains a cryptographic hash of the previous block, creating an unbreakable chain. Even if someone tries to alter a transaction in an earlier block, the hash values of all subsequent blocks will change, making the tampering immediately detectable by the network.

This decentralised structure gives blockchains their security and transparency. Instead of relying on a central authority, the network of miners and nodes (computers participating in the network) collectively maintains and validates the blockchain, ensuring its integrity.

The Basics of Cryptography in Cryptocurrencies

Cryptocurrencies like Bitcoin depend on advanced cryptographic techniques to secure transactions and protect user identities. Public-key cryptography, also known as asymmetric cryptography, is at the core of this security.

Every cryptocurrency user has a pair of cryptographic keys: a public key and a private key. The public key is used to receive funds, while the private key authorises and signs transactions. This system guarantees that only the legitimate owner of a cryptocurrency can access and spend their funds.

When a transaction is initiated, the sender's private key is used to create a digital signature, which is then attached to the transaction. The network nodes can then use the sender's public key to verify the signature's authenticity, confirming that the rightful owner authorised the transaction.

This cryptographic process makes cryptocurrencies secure and decentralised, eliminating the need for a central authority to validate transactions.

Smart Contracts and Their Potential (Ethereum as an Example)

While Bitcoin pioneered the use of blockchain technology for digital currency, other cryptocurrencies, such as Ethereum, have expanded blockchain's capabilities by introducing Smart Contracts.

Smart contracts are self-executing digital agreements that automatically enforce the terms of a contract when certain conditions are met. They are stored on the blockchain and can be programmed to handle a wide range of transactions and interactions, from simple payments to complex financial instruments and decentralised applications (dApps).

For example, a Smart Contract could automatically transfer ownership of a digital asset once a payment is received, eliminating the need for a third-party intermediary.

Ethereum, the second-largest cryptocurrency by market capitalisation, is particularly well-known for its Smart Contract functionality. Ethereum's blockchain allows developers to create and deploy their own decentralised applications, which can be used for various purposes, such as decentralised finance (DeFi), non-fungible tokens (NFTs), and decentralised autonomous organisations (DAOs).

The potential of Smart Contracts is fascinating. Their ability to automate and streamline various processes, reduce the need for intermediaries, and increase transparency and trust in transactions is a game-changer. As the Ethereum network and other blockchain platforms continue to evolve, the applications of Smart Contracts are expected to expand, offering new investment opportunities and use cases.

Proof of Work vs. Proof of Stake

Proof of Work (PoW) and Proof of Stake (PoS) are common consensus mechanisms in cryptocurrencies.

As seen in Bitcoin, Proof of Work requires miners to solve complex mathematical problems to validate transactions and add new blocks to the blockchain. This process consumes a significant amount of computational power and energy as miners compete to be the first to solve the problem and receive a reward in the form of newly minted cryptocurrency.

On the other hand, Proof of Stake, as used by Ethereum 2.0 and other cryptocurrencies, relies on users who already hold the cryptocurrency to validate transactions. These users, known as validators, must "stake" a portion of their holdings to participate in the validation process. The more a user stakes, the more likely they will be selected to validate a block and earn a reward.

The main difference between these two consensus mechanisms is how they ensure the security and integrity of the blockchain. Proof of Work relies on computational power, where miners compete to solve complex mathematical problems to validate transactions and add new blocks to the blockchain.

On the other hand, Proof of Stake relies on economic incentives, where users who already hold the cryptocurrency are selected to validate transactions based on the amount of cryptocurrency they 'stake' or lock up as collateral. Each approach has its advantages and trade-offs, which can impact the cryptocurrency network's scalability, energy efficiency, and decentralisation.

Relating Technical Knowledge to Investment Decisions

Understanding the technical aspects of cryptocurrencies is about more than just knowledge. It's about empowerment. By grasping the foundational blockchain technology, cryptographic principles, and consensus mechanisms, investors can better assess the strengths, weaknesses, and long-term potential of different cryptocurrencies, empowering them to make informed decisions.

Understanding the trade-offs between Proof of Work and Proof of Stake is not just about understanding the technicalities; it's about understanding the complexities of cryptocurrency. This knowledge can help evaluate a cryptocurrency's energy efficiency, scalability, and decentralisation—all of which are crucial factors for determining its sustainability and growth potential.

While not essential for successful cryptocurrency investments, technical knowledge can provide a deeper understanding of the technology and help investors make more informed decisions based on their goals and risk tolerance.

Coins vs. Tokens: Knowing the Difference

Coins are digital currencies that operate on their own blockchain. They are primarily used as a medium of exchange, a store of value, or a unit of account. Bitcoin (BTC), the first and most well-known cryptocurrency, and other currencies like Ethereum (ETH), which has its own blockchain supporting a broader range of functionalities, are examples of coins.

Tokens are digital assets built on top of another cryptocurrency's blockchain. They can represent various assets or rights managed by a smart contract and the underlying blockchain. Tokens often serve specific purposes within decentralised applications (dApps) or ecosystems, such as granting access to services, serving as a stake in governance decisions, or representing physical assets in a digital form. An example is the ERC-20 tokens on the Ethereum network.

Initial Coin Offerings (ICOs) and Token Sales

Initial Coin Offerings (ICOs) and token sales are methods used by blockchain projects to raise capital by issuing digital tokens. ICOs involve selling a new cryptocurrency token to early investors in exchange for established cryptocurrencies like Bitcoin or Ethereum. These tokens typically represent a stake in the project or provide access to its services. On the other hand, token sales may offer utility tokens that grant access to a platform or service.

In addition to ICOs and token sales, Initial Exchange Offerings (IEOs) have emerged as a popular alternative. IEOs are conducted on cryptocurrency exchanges, which act as intermediaries and manage the token sale process on behalf of the issuing project. The exchange performs due diligence on the project, providing investors with additional trust and security. IEOs typically offer more streamlined and secure fundraising processes, as the exchange handles the logistics of the token sale, including user verification (KYC/AML), and provides a ready-made platform for token distribution.

Before investing in ICOs, token sales, or IEOs, investors should thoroughly research the project, including its whitepaper, team members, roadmap, and tokenomics. Due diligence is crucial to assess the project's viability, potential for growth, and the legitimacy of the offering. Knowing the risks associated with investing in these types of sales, such as regulatory uncertainties, project failures, and potential scams, is essential.

Understanding the mechanics of ICOs, IEOs, and token sales can help investors make informed decisions and navigate the evolving landscape of blockchain fundraising.

Tokenomics and Utility Tokens

Tokenomics, the economic model that governs the creation, distribution, and management of tokens within a blockchain ecosystem, is a crucial concept for investors. Understanding tokenomics empowers investors to evaluate the usefulness and value of digital assets. Utility tokens, a type of cryptocurrency, serve specific functions within decentralised applications (dApps) or blockchain ecosystems.

Utility tokens are not just a type of cryptocurrency, they are a key that unlocks access to platform services, enables participation in governance decisions, and represents ownership of digital assets. Their value is derived from their usefulness within the ecosystem and the demand for the services or products they enable. When investors assess utility tokens, they consider factors such as the project's roadmap, token distribution, use cases, and community adoption.

Analysing tokenomics is a powerful tool for investors, enabling them to identify projects with strong fundamentals, sustainable token economics, and a promising potential for long-term growth. Evaluating utility tokens requires a deep understanding of the token's purpose, its usefulness within the ecosystem, and the project's ability to deliver on its promises.

Decentralisation: The Core Philosophy

Decentralisation is a hallmark of cryptocurrencies, challenging traditional centralised financial systems. In a decentralised system, decisions and operations are distributed across the network rather than controlled by a single entity (like a central bank). This approach aims to reduce points of failure, increase transparency, and give users more control over their assets.

Making Informed Investment Decisions

Armed with an understanding of these basics, investors can better navigate the cryptocurrency market. Here are a few tips for applying this knowledge to investment decisions:

- **Evaluate Technological Potential**: Look beyond price fluctuations and market trends. Investigate the technology behind a cryptocurrency, its use cases, and how it addresses specific problems or creates value.

- **Assess the Team and Community Support**: The strength and transparency of the development team and active community support can be indicators of a project's credibility and long-term viability.

- **Understand Market Dynamics**: Cryptocurrency markets are influenced by a wide range of factors, including technological developments, regulatory news, and market sentiment.

  Keeping informed can help an investor anticipate market movements.

- **Diversifying Portfolio**: Given the variety of coins and tokens available, consider diversifying the investments to spread risk. However, ensure each investment is based on thorough research and understanding of the asset.
- **Stay Informed and Cautious**: The cryptocurrency market is fast-evolving, with new technologies and projects emerging regularly. Continuous learning and a cautious approach can help mitigate risks.

Conclusion

In this chapter, we have explored the fundamental concepts of cryptocurrencies and blockchain technology, laying the groundwork for informed investment decisions. Understanding the core principles of decentralisation, the differences between coins and tokens, and the technical aspects of consensus mechanisms is crucial for evaluating the actual value and potential of various digital assets.

Investors can make more informed choices that align with their financial goals and risk tolerance by looking beyond market hype and focusing on the underlying technology. Recognising the significance of decentralisation and how it challenges traditional financial systems provides valuable context for navigating the cryptocurrency market.

Additionally, grasping the technical nuances of Proof of Work and Proof of Stake consensus mechanisms can help investors assess the security, scalability, and environmental impact of different cryptocurrency networks. This knowledge empowers investors to look beyond surface-level factors and make more strategic investment decisions.

Equipped with a solid understanding of the basics, investors can now explore more advanced topics and strategies covered in the subsequent chapters of this comprehensive guide. The foundation laid in this chapter will serve as a springboard for a successful and informed cryptocurrency investment journey.

Questions & Answers

Q   What is the significance of understanding cryptocurrencies and blockchain technology in the context of investments?

    A   Understanding cryptocurrencies and blockchain technology is crucial for making informed investment decisions in the crypto market. This knowledge allows investors to look beyond market hype and evaluate the true value and potential of different digital assets.

Q   How do coins and tokens differ, and why is it important for investors to know this distinction?

    A   Coins are used as digital currency, while tokens have various functionalities within blockchain ecosystems. Understanding this difference is important for investors to properly assess the utility and potential of different cryptocurrency projects.

Q   What are the core benefits of decentralisation in cryptocurrencies, and how does it impact traditional financial systems?

    A   Decentralisation offers increased transparency, security, and control to users, challenging traditional centralised systems. This shift empowers individuals and reduces the influence of central authorities.

Q   Why is decentralisation considered a core philosophy in cryptocurrency investments?

    A   Decentralisation aligns with the fundamental principles of cryptocurrencies, promoting transparency and user empowerment. This philosophy is a key factor in the appeal and growth of the cryptocurrency market.

Q   How do Proof of Work (PoW) and Proof of Stake (PoS) consensus mechanisms differ, and what are the implications for investors?

    A   PoW requires miners to solve complex mathematical problems to validate transactions, while PoS relies on users who already hold the cryptocurrency to validate transactions based on the amount they hold. Understanding these differences can help investors evaluate the security, scalability, and energy efficiency of various cryptocurrency networks.

Q What are the key considerations for evaluating the technological potential of a cryptocurrency project?

    A Investors should look beyond price fluctuations and market trends, and instead focus on factors such as the project's underlying technology, the strength of the development team, and the real-world applications and use cases of the cryptocurrency.

Chapter 2

Setting the Investment Goals

Define the Investment Horizon

- **Short-term**: Involves buying and selling cryptocurrencies within a short period, such as days, weeks, or a few months.

- **Medium-term**: Holding positions for several months to a year.

- **Long-term**: Investing with a horizon of several years, focusing on the fundamental value and long-term potential of cryptocurrencies.

When venturing into the world of cryptocurrency trading, one of the most crucial decisions an investor will need to make is defining their investment horizon. This term refers to the length of time the investor plans to hold onto their investments before selling them. The choice of an investment horizon can significantly influence the investor's trading strategy, risk tolerance, and the types of cryptocurrencies they might choose to invest in at any period. Here is a more in-depth look at the three primary investment horizons:

Short-term Investing

Short-term investing involves buying and selling cryptocurrencies within a relatively brief period, ranging from a few days to several weeks or, at most, a few months. This approach is akin to sprinting; it is fast-paced, requires constant attention, and aims to capitalise on short-term market fluctuations.

Characteristics and Strategies:

- **High Volatility:** Short-term traders thrive on the cryptocurrency market's volatility. They aim to profit from rapid price changes.

- **Active Trading:** Requires frequent market monitoring to make timely decisions. Many short-term traders use technical analysis and trading indicators to identify potential buy or sell signals.

- **Day Trading and Scalping:** Common strategies include day trading, where all positions are closed before the market closes to avoid overnight market volatility, and scalping, which involves making numerous trades throughout the day to capture small price gaps.

Medium-term Investing

Medium-term investing involves holding onto cryptocurrencies for several months up to a year. This approach is similar to running a middle-distance race—not a sprint, but not a marathon. The goal is to achieve noticeable growth, not the quick wins of day trading.

Characteristics and Strategies:

- **Market Trends:** Medium-term investors often base their decisions on broader market trends rather than short-term fluctuations. They might use a combination of technical and fundamental analysis to pick investments that show promise over the next few months.

- **Swing Trading:** Common strategy for medium-term investors. It involves taking advantage of market 'swings' or cycles, buying during downturns, and selling during upswings.

Long-term Investing

Long-term investing involves holding cryptocurrencies for several years and focusing on their fundamental value and the long-term potential of the technology behind them. This approach is more like a marathon, requiring patience, vision, and a strong belief in the underlying principles of the assets being held.

Characteristics and Strategies:

1. **Fundamental Analysis:** Long-term investors deeply analyse the potential of a cryptocurrency's underlying technology, use case, team, and market position. They invest in assets they believe will grow significantly over the years.

2. **HODLing:** A popular term in the crypto community, "HODL" (a misspelling of "hold") refers to the strategy of holding onto investments regardless of short-term market fluctuations.

3. **Diversification:** Long-term investors often diversify their portfolios across different cryptocurrencies and asset classes to mitigate risks.

Choosing an Investment Horizon

One's choice among these investment horizons should reflect one's financial goals, risk tolerance, and the time one can dedicate to monitoring one's investments.

- Short-term investing might offer quick returns but comes with high risk and requires a lot of time and attention.

- Medium-term investing balances the intensive nature of short-term trading and the patience required for long-term holding, offering a middle ground for those looking to avoid daily market volatility.

- Long-term investing, on the other hand, is suited for those with a strong belief in the future of cryptocurrencies and the patience to wait out the market's ups and downs.

In summary, defining one's investment horizon is a foundational step in crafting a cryptocurrency trading strategy that aligns with one's goals, lifestyle, and risk tolerance.

Calculating the Investment Amount

Investors should invest only funds they can afford to lose. They should consider their earnings, savings, monthly expenses, and future commitments and allocate a percentage of their disposable income to cryptocurrencies, ensuring they do not hinder their financial stability.

When considering an investment in cryptocurrencies, it is crucial to approach it with a clear understanding of their financial situation and risk tolerance. Cryptocurrencies are known for their volatility, which can lead to significant gains but also substantial losses. Therefore, deciding on the amount to invest requires careful consideration of several factors:

1. **Evaluate the Financial Health**

   Before allocating any funds to cryptocurrency investments, investors should conduct a thorough assessment of their financial health. This includes understanding their income streams, monthly expenses, existing savings, debts, and any future financial obligations they might have (such as loans, mortgage payments, or planned large purchases). The goal is to ensure that their investment will maintain their ability to meet their essential needs and financial commitments.

2. **Understand the Investment Goals**

   A person's investment goals play a significant role in determining how much they should invest in cryptocurrencies. Whether they are looking to make a quick profit or are interested in the long-term potential of blockchain technology, their goals will influence not only the amount they invest but also the types of cryptocurrencies they might consider.

3. **Assess the Risk Tolerance**

   Risk tolerance refers to the degree of variability in investment returns an individual is willing to withstand. Cryptocurrency markets can be highly unpredictable, with prices fluctuating wildly in short periods. If one is risk-averse, they should allocate a smaller portion of their portfolio to cryptocurrencies. Conversely, someone with a higher risk tolerance might be comfortable with a larger investment, understanding that there's a potential for higher returns alongside the risk of significant losses.

4. **Determine the Disposable Income**
   Disposable income is the amount of money a person has left after paying taxes and necessary living expenses. Individuals need to invest only a portion of their disposable income in cryptocurrencies, ensuring that they have enough left to cover unexpected expenses without needing to liquidate their investment prematurely, possibly resulting in a loss.

5. **Follow the Principle of Diversification**
   Diversification is a risk management strategy that involves spreading one's investments across various assets to reduce exposure to any single asset or risk. Even within cryptocurrency investments, it's recommended to consider diversifying across different coins and tokens to mitigate risk. It's essential to remember that diversification can't eliminate risk entirely but can help manage it more effectively.

6. **Setting Aside an Emergency Fund**
   Before investing in cryptocurrencies, one should ensure that they have an emergency fund in place. It is recommended to have a readily accessible sum of money that can cover at least 3-6 months of living expenses in case of unexpected financial difficulties. An emergency fund ensures that one won't have to dip into their investments, which could be detrimental in a volatile market.

7. **Continuously Re-evaluate the Investment**
   The cryptocurrency market is dynamic, with new developments and changes occurring regularly. As such, it's important for investors to periodically reassess their investment amount in line with changes in their financial situation, investment goals, and the market landscape. They should be prepared to adjust their investment strategy as necessary.

In summary, deciding on the amount to invest in cryptocurrencies requires a balanced approach considering an investor's financial health, goals, risk tolerance, and the principles of diversification and emergency preparedness.

By carefully evaluating these factors, investors can make informed decisions that align with their financial situation and investment objectives, helping to ensure that their foray into cryptocurrency investing is both responsible and aligned with their broader financial plan.

Conclusion

Investors venturing into cryptocurrency trading should understand and define their investment horizons as a critical step. By categorising their investments into short-term, medium-term, and long-term horizons, they can tailor strategies to match their financial goals, risk tolerance, and the time available for managing their portfolios.

Choosing the right investment horizon, alongside a careful calculation of investment amounts based on financial health and objectives, will enable investors to navigate the volatile world of cryptocurrencies more confidently and effectively. This strategic approach ensures that their investments align with their overall financial plans and helps mitigate potential risks associated with cryptocurrency trading.

Questions & Answers

Q What factors should investors consider when defining their investment horizon?

    A Factors include financial goals, risk tolerance, and time commitment.

Q How do short-term investing characteristics differ from medium-term and long-term investing?

    A Short-term investing involves quick trades, while medium- and long-term investing focuses on different timeframes and strategies.

Q Why is calculating the investment amount important in setting investment goals?

    A Calculating the investment amount ensures alignment with financial objectives and risk tolerance.

Q How does choosing the right investment horizon impact an investor's overall strategy?

    A The investment horizon determines the approach to trading, risk management, and portfolio diversification.

Chapter 3

Portfolio Management and Diversification

Portfolio management and diversification are fundamental principles in the realm of investments, and they hold particular importance in the volatile and unpredictable world of cryptocurrency. Diversification aims not necessarily to maximise returns (though it can lead to that) but rather to mitigate risk by spreading investments across various assets. This strategy can help ensure that the negative performance of one investment doesn't disproportionately affect the portfolio's overall health.

Here's a deeper look into how diversification can be applied effectively in cryptocurrency investments and trading:

Understanding Diversification in Cryptocurrency

In the context of cryptocurrency, diversification means not putting all the funds into a single digital currency or token. The crypto market is known for its rapid and unpredictable price fluctuations. By diversifying investments across different cryptocurrencies, investors can reduce the impact of a significant price drop in any single cryptocurrency on their overall portfolio.

Criteria for Diversifying the Crypto Portfolio

1. **Market Capitalisation**: Cryptocurrencies with a higher market cap are generally considered less risky than those with a smaller market cap.

Bitcoin (BTC) and Ethereum (ETH) are examples of high-market-cap cryptocurrencies that many investors consider "safer" bets. However, they can still be volatile and carry risks.

2. **Technological Innovation and Use Cases**: Look for cryptocurrencies that offer unique technological advancements or solve specific problems. These could include faster transaction speeds, improved security features, or novel consensus mechanisms. A cryptocurrency's utility in real-world applications can be a good indicator of its potential longevity and success.

3. **Development Team and Community Support**: A strong, active, and transparent development team, along with a supportive and engaged community, can be crucial factors in the success of a cryptocurrency project. They indicate the project's credibility and the likelihood of continued development and improvement.

4. **Promising Altcoins**: While Bitcoin and Ethereum are the most well-known, thousands of altcoins might offer good investment opportunities. Some of these could be in niches such as decentralised finance (DeFi), non-fungible tokens (NFTs), or smart contracts. Researching and investing in promising altcoins can yield high returns, but they often come with higher risks.

Strategies for Diversification

1. **Sector Diversification**: Cryptocurrencies can be categorised into different sectors based on their use cases, such as DeFi, NFTs, smart contracts, privacy coins, and more. Investing across different sectors can help spread risk.

2. **Geographic Diversification**: Considering projects based in different countries or regions can also be a form of diversification, as it spreads the geopolitical risk that might affect the regulatory environment of the cryptocurrency.

3. **Time Diversification**: The strategy of spreading investments over time, known as dollar-cost averaging, involves investing smaller amounts regularly instead of a lump sum at once. This can help reduce the impact of volatility.

Implementing the Diversification Strategy

1. **Research**: Conduct thorough research on various cryptocurrencies, understanding their market potential, technological foundation, and the problems they aim to solve.

2. **Assessment**: Individuals are advised to regularly assess and rebalance their investment portfolios to ensure that they align with their risk tolerance and investment goals. This may involve reallocating profits from one investment to another.

3. **Stay Informed**: The cryptocurrency market is constantly evolving. Staying informed about market trends, technological developments, and regulatory changes is crucial for maintaining a diversified and balanced portfolio.

Exploring Alternative Investment Options in Cryptocurrencies

In addition to DeFi and centralised exchanges, investors have various alternative investment options in the cryptocurrency market. Initial coin offerings (ICOs) and security token offerings (STOs) are fundraising methods used by blockchain projects to raise capital by issuing tokens. ICOs involve the sale of utility tokens, while STOs offer security tokens backed by real-world assets.

Cryptocurrency mining is another alternative investment method where miners validate transactions on a blockchain network in exchange for rewards. Each alternative investment option comes with its own set of risks and potential rewards. For example, ICOs may carry regulatory risks, while mining requires technical expertise and investment in mining equipment.

Investors should carefully research and assess the risks before engaging in alternative investment methods to diversify their cryptocurrency portfolio.

Conclusion

In summary, diversification in cryptocurrency investing is a strategic approach to managing risk and seeking balanced returns. By carefully selecting a mix of cryptocurrencies based on thorough research and strategic criteria, investors can navigate the volatile crypto market with greater confidence and resilience.

Questions & Answers

Q Why is diversification essential in managing a cryptocurrency portfolio?

    A Diversification helps spread risk and optimise returns by investing in various assets.

Q What criteria should investors consider when diversifying their crypto portfolio?

    A Criteria include asset types, market sectors, and risk levels.

Q How can investors implement an effective diversification strategy in their portfolios?

    A Implementing a diversification strategy involves selecting a mix of assets based on research and risk assessment.

Q What are the alternative investment options available in the cryptocurrency market for diversification?

    A Alternative options include ICOs, STOs, and cryptocurrency mining.

Q How does diversification help investors navigate the volatile cryptocurrency market?

    A Diversification minimises the impact of market fluctuations on the overall portfolio performance.

Chapter 4

Environmental Impact of Cryptocurrency Mining

Sustainable Practices and Strategic Insights

Cryptocurrency is gaining popularity worldwide, but its mining processes are causing concern over its environmental impact. Mining for coins like Bitcoin requires significant computational power and energy consumption, which raises questions about the process's sustainability and environmental footprint. This has become a significant topic of discussion among investors, regulators, and the general public.

Understanding the Environmental Impact

Cryptocurrency mining requires a lot of energy. It involves using specialised hardware, such as ASICs or GPUs, to solve complex mathematical problems that validate transactions and secure the blockchain. This process, known as proof-of-work (PoW), consumes a significant amount of electricity, which is often generated using fossil fuels. As a result, it leads to considerable carbon emissions.

Geographic Impact and Energy Sources

The environmental impact of mining operations varies considerably based on their geographic location. Regions that rely heavily on non-renewable energy sources like coal for electricity generate a higher environmental impact than areas powered by renewable energy sources. Therefore, selecting the location for mining operations is critical in determining the overall carbon footprint of the cryptocurrencies mined.

Shift Towards Renewable Energy

The industry is noticing a shift towards renewable energy sources in response to growing environmental concerns. Mining operations are increasingly powered by solar, wind, and hydroelectric power, reducing the carbon footprint and promoting more sustainable growth of cryptocurrencies. Investors prefer companies prioritising green energy sources, reflecting a broader trend towards environmentally responsible investing.

Innovations in Mining Technology

Technological advancements are crucial in reducing the environmental impact of cryptocurrency mining. Innovations, such as more energy-efficient mining hardware and improvements in cooling technologies, can decrease the overall energy consumption of mining operations.

Some blockchain networks are also exploring alternatives to PoW, such as proof-of-stake (PoS), Delegated Proof of Stake (DPoS) and proof-of-space. These alternatives require significantly less energy to maintain network security and integrity.

Regulatory and Investor Influence

Regulators and investors are becoming more conscious of the environmental impact caused by cryptocurrency mining. They are now advocating for sustainable practices in the sector. Some of the measures being taken include encouraging renewable energy usage through incentives and regulations and penalising mining operations with a high environmental impact.

Investors are now advised to invest in companies that prioritise sustainable mining practices. This not only aligns with ethical values but also mitigates potential regulatory risks.

The Role of Community and Transparency

Transparency in reporting energy consumption and sources used in cryptocurrency mining is increasingly vital. Investors and consumers demand more transparency, leading companies to adopt more sustainable practices. Community initiatives and collaborations aimed at reducing the environmental impact of mining are also gaining momentum, creating a more sustainable ecosystem for cryptocurrencies.

Conclusion

The impact of cryptocurrency mining on the environment is a significant issue that requires collective action to address. By understanding the impact, shifting towards the use of renewable energy, innovating in technology, and influencing regulatory and investment decisions, the cryptocurrency industry can move towards a more sustainable future. It's important for investors to stay informed about these practices for ethical investing and to ensure the long-term viability and acceptance of cryptocurrencies in an increasingly environmentally conscious global economy.

Questions & Answers

Q **What is the significance of understanding the environmental impact of cryptocurrency mining?**

A Understanding the environmental impact is crucial for promoting sustainable practices and addressing concerns related to energy consumption and carbon emissions.

Q **How does the geographic location of mining operations impact the environmental footprint of cryptocurrencies?**

A The geographic location influences the environmental impact based on the energy sources used, with regions relying on renewable energy sources having a lower carbon footprint.

Q **What is the role of renewable energy sources in addressing the environmental impact of cryptocurrency mining?**

A The shift towards renewable energy sources helps reduce the carbon footprint of mining operations, promoting sustainability and environmental responsibility.

Q **How do innovations in mining technology contribute to reducing the environmental impact of cryptocurrency mining?**

A Innovations such as energy-efficient mining hardware and alternative consensus mechanisms can decrease energy consumption and promote eco-friendly mining practices.

Chapter 5

Staking and Yield Farming

Opportunities for Passive Income in Cryptocurrency Markets

In the rapidly changing world of cryptocurrency, traders and investors always seek ways to maximise their returns beyond traditional buying and selling. Two popular methods for earning passive income are staking and yield farming, which offer additional avenues for investors to make the most of their crypto holdings. A clear understanding of these concepts can be crucial for those seeking to diversify their investment strategies and enhance their earnings from digital assets.

Staking: Securing Networks while Earning Rewards

Staking refers to the act of holding funds in a cryptocurrency wallet to support the operations and security of a blockchain network. This method is commonly used in blockchain networks that use a Proof of Stake (PoS) or one of its variants (such as Delegated Proof of Stake or DPoS) as their consensus mechanism. Investors can participate in network operations such as transaction validation or voting on governance decisions by staking their coins.

Benefits of Staking:

- **Regular Rewards**: Investors who stake their cryptocurrencies receive rewards, typically in the form of additional coins or tokens. These rewards are analogous to interest payouts, providing a steady income stream.

- **Enhanced Security**: More stakers on the blockchain network lead to increased stability and security, as staking enhances efficiency.

- **Low Energy Consumption**: Unlike Proof of Work (PoW) systems, PoS does not require extensive computational power, making staking a more environmentally friendly option.

Considerations:

- **Lock-up Periods**: Some networks may require funds to be locked up for a designated period, during which they cannot be traded. This can be a disadvantage during periods of high volatility.

- **Slashing Risks**: In specific networks, stakers may face penalties, known as "slashes," if they validate incorrect transactions or engage in other actions deemed harmful to the network.

Yield Farming: Leveraging Crypto Assets for Higher Returns

Yield farming, also called liquidity mining, is a process where cryptocurrency assets are lent out to earn high returns from trading fees in the form of additional cryptocurrency. This practice is predominantly observed in the decentralised finance (DeFi) sector, where investors automate the lending and borrowing processes through smart contracts.

Benefits of Yield Farming:

- **High Potential Returns**: Yield farming is a strategy that can provide much higher returns than traditional staking. However, it also involves higher risks.

- **Compounding Returns**: Farmers can benefit from the compounding effect by reinvesting their earnings.

- **Diversification**: Investors can farm different pools to spread out risk and increase exposure to various DeFi projects.

Considerations:

- **Complexity**: DeFi yield farming strategies can be complex and require a comprehensive understanding of associated protocols.

- **Impermanent Loss**: If the price of staked tokens changes after the deposit, investors may experience impermanent loss, particularly during volatile markets.

- **Smart Contract Risks**: Smart contracts used in yield farming can be vulnerable to bugs and errors, which may result in significant losses.

Conclusion

Cryptocurrency traders and investors interested in diversifying their portfolio strategies may consider staking and yield farming as viable options to generate passive income. Investors should be aware of the risks associated with both of these methods.

Thorough research and understanding of each approach's mechanisms and potential pitfalls are crucial. By carefully selecting their investments and strategies, investors can effectively enhance their participation in the flourishing field of cryptocurrencies, which could lead to improved financial outcomes in their trading endeavours.

Questions & Answers

Q What is the purpose of staking in the cryptocurrency market?

A Staking involves securing blockchain networks and earning rewards by holding and validating digital assets.

Q What are the benefits of staking for cryptocurrency investors?

A Staking offers passive income opportunities, network security, and potential participant rewards.

Q What considerations should investors keep in mind when engaging in staking?

A Considerations include lock-up periods, technical requirements, and potential risks associated with staking.

Q How does yield farming differ from traditional investment methods?

A Yield farming involves leveraging crypto assets to earn higher returns through various DeFi protocols and liquidity pools.

Q What advantages does yield farming offer to investors?

A Yield farming provides opportunities for increased returns, token incentives, and participation in decentralised finance projects.

Q What factors should investors consider before participating in yield farming?

A Factors include understanding smart contract risks, liquidity provision, and the overall DeFi ecosystem.

Chapter 6

Understanding Cryptocurrency ETFs

Cryptocurrency Exchange-Traded Funds (ETFs) are a ground-breaking development in digital asset investment. They serve as a link between conventional financial markets and the constantly evolving cryptocurrency industry. ETFs simplify the complexities of direct ownership by providing investors with a more familiar and regulated way to gain exposure to cryptocurrencies.

Introduction to Cryptocurrency ETFs

A cryptocurrency ETF is an investment fund traded on stock exchanges, similar to traditional ETFs. It tracks the performance of one or more digital tokens, allowing investors to mirror the price movements of cryptocurrencies like Bitcoin, Ethereum or a basket of digital assets. By investing in a cryptocurrency ETF, investors can buy and sell shares of the ETF through traditional brokerage accounts. This way, they can bypass the need to deal with cryptocurrency exchanges or secure digital wallets.

Benefits of Investing in Cryptocurrency ETFs

1. **Simplified Investment Process:** Investors can trade cryptocurrency ETFs using their existing brokerage accounts, eliminating the need to navigate the often complex landscape of cryptocurrency exchanges.

   Buying and selling shares in a cryptocurrency ETF is as straightforward as trading any other ETF or stock, making it accessible even to those with limited knowledge of cryptocurrencies.

2. **Regulatory Oversight:** Cryptocurrency ETFs must comply with regulatory frameworks in the jurisdictions in which they are offered. Such oversight provides a layer of security and credibility that direct cryptocurrency investments lack, reducing the risk of fraud and mismanagement.

3. **Diversification:** Some cryptocurrency ETFs allow investors to diversify their holdings in the crypto space without managing multiple digital assets.

4. **Reduced Risk of Theft:** Investing in a cryptocurrency ETF eliminates the need to hold digital currencies directly, thereby mitigating the risk of wallet hacks and cryptographic key theft.

Considerations Before Investing in Cryptocurrency ETFs

1. **Expense Ratios and Fees:** Cryptocurrency ETFs can affect overall returns due to management fees and expense ratios. Investors need to review these costs as they would with any other ETF.

2. **Market Volatility:** The value of cryptocurrencies is highly volatile. Although ETFs offer some insulation by pooling multiple assets, their underlying value can still fluctuate significantly.

3. **Liquidity:** The liquidity of a cryptocurrency ETF depends on the market demand for the ETF shares and the liquidity of the underlying digital assets. Liquidity challenges can arise in stressful market conditions.

4. **Tracking Errors:** An ETF may experience tracking errors when it fails to replicate its underlying assets' performance accurately. These discrepancies can arise due to timing differences, fees, or the management strategies employed by the ETF.

How to Invest in Cryptocurrency ETFs

1. **Brokerage Account:** Investors must have an active brokerage account to purchase and sell ETFs. It is crucial to opt for a brokerage firm that

offers a wide range of ETFs, including cryptocurrency ETFs, and has competitive trading fees.

2. **Research and Selection:** Individuals interested in investing in cryptocurrency ETFs should conduct thorough research to understand the investment goals, strategies, and the particular cryptocurrencies included in the ETF. One way to obtain this information is to review the ETF's prospectus, which is a document that provides details on the investment strategy, risks, and expenses associated with the ETF.

3. **Monitoring and Rebalancing:** Like any other investment, it is essential to regularly review and adjust the holdings of a cryptocurrency ETF to match the investor's risk appetite and investment goals. The market conditions and performance of individual cryptocurrencies can change over time, which may affect the suitability of an ETF investment. Therefore, keeping track of these changes is necessary to make informed decisions about the ETF portfolio.

Conclusion

Investors keen on venturing into the cryptocurrency market can consider investing in Cryptocurrency ETFs, which offer a regulated and familiar investment vehicle. These ETFs offer several benefits, such as ease of use, diversification, and reduced risk of theft. However, investors should also be aware of the fees, volatility, and liquidity issues associated with these products.

To effectively incorporate cryptocurrency ETFs into their broader investment strategy, investors must conduct thorough research and adopt a proactive approach to portfolio management. This could enhance both the diversification and the performance of their investment portfolios.

Questions & Answers

Q What is the purpose of introducing cryptocurrency ETFs to investors?

    A Cryptocurrency ETFs provide a convenient way for investors to gain exposure to digital assets without directly owning them.

Q What benefits do investors gain from investing in cryptocurrency ETFs?

    A Benefits include diversification, regulatory oversight, and simplified access to the cryptocurrency market.

Q What considerations should investors evaluate before investing in cryptocurrency ETFs?

    A Considerations include regulatory compliance, fees, liquidity, and the underlying assets of the ETF.

Q How can investors invest in cryptocurrency ETFs?

    A Investors can access cryptocurrency ETFs through traditional brokerage accounts or specialised ETF trading platforms.

Q Why is it important for investors to understand the regulatory landscape of cryptocurrency ETFs?

    A Understanding regulations ensures compliance, reduces risks and enhances transparency in cryptocurrency investments.

Chapter 7

Risk Management Strategies

Introduction to Risk Management

Risk management is a critical component of successful cryptocurrency investing. The crypto market is known for its high volatility and unpredictability, which can lead to substantial gains and significant losses.

Effective risk management involves identifying potential risks, assessing their likelihood and impact, and implementing mitigation strategies.

This proactive approach helps protect investment capital while maximising the profit potential.
Understanding the types of risks, such as market, liquidity, and regulatory risks, and how they can affect investments is the first step in developing a robust risk management strategy.

Setting Stop-Loss Orders

A stop-loss order is a tool that investors use to limit potential losses on a cryptocurrency position. When setting a stop-loss, investors instruct their trading platform to sell an asset when it reaches a specific price, thus preventing further losses if the market moves against them.

The key to setting effective stop-loss orders is understanding risk tolerance—how much of their capital investors are willing to risk on a single trade. Additionally, it is crucial to consider the volatility of the cryptocurrency and the overall market conditions.

For instance, setting too tight a stop-loss in a highly volatile market could lead to premature sales of assets. Conversely, too loose a setting might result in unnecessary losses. Based on technical analysis and recent market behaviour, strategic placement of stop-loss orders can significantly help manage investment risks.

Leverage Management

Leverage in cryptocurrency trading allows investors to control larger positions than their current capital would ordinarily permit. While this can amplify profits, it also increases the risk of substantial losses, potentially exceeding initial investments.

Managing leverage effectively involves understanding the leverage ratio, which indicates how much more investors are trading than their actual investment. For example, a 10:1 leverage ratio means they are trading ten times the amount of their capital. It is also essential to be aware of the margin requirements set by exchanges, which can vary and affect trading capacity.

A prudent approach to leverage involves using it sparingly and adjusting according to the market's state and comfort with potential losses.

Diversification Across Asset Classes

Diversification is a foundational strategy in risk management and applies to cryptocurrency investing. By spreading investments across various crypto assets, such as Bitcoin, Ethereum, altcoins, and even different sectors like DeFi, NFTs, and more, investors can reduce the impact of a decline in any single asset or market segment.

This strategy helps smooth out returns and reduce the volatility of their portfolio. Moreover, considering investments outside of cryptocurrencies, such as traditional stocks, bonds, or real estate, can further diversify and stabilise their investment portfolio.

Case Studies in Risk Management

Real-world examples serve as valuable lessons in the effectiveness of risk management strategies. For instance, during the 2018 cryptocurrency bear market, investors who had diversified portfolios and used stop-loss orders mitigated losses better than those who were heavily invested in single assets without protective measures.

Another example could be the use of dynamic leverage management during the March 2020 market crash, where investors who adjusted their leverage in response to increasing volatility were able to avoid margin calls and catastrophic losses.

These case studies underline the importance of adaptive and well-planned risk management strategies in navigating the complex and volatile cryptocurrency markets.

Cryptocurrency Investment Scams

Investors in the digital asset space must proactively protect their funds and make informed decisions. Cryptocurrency investment scams, such as Ponzi schemes, fake initial coin offerings (ICOs), phishing attacks, and fraudulent investment platforms, pose significant risks. Understanding common scam tactics and red flags is crucial to navigating the cryptocurrency market with confidence.

One of the most effective ways to avoid falling victim to cryptocurrency scams is to be cautious of schemes that promise high returns with little to no risk, unsolicited offers, and pressure tactics to invest quickly. However, the key to staying safe in the digital asset space is conducting thorough research, verifying the legitimacy of projects, and steering clear of investments that seem too good to be true.

Conclusion

In conclusion, effective risk management is indispensable for cryptocurrency investors aiming to navigate the volatile and unpredictable nature of the crypto market. Investors can significantly mitigate potential losses and protect their capital by understanding and implementing key strategies such as setting stop-loss orders, managing leverage, diversifying across asset classes, and learning from real-world case studies. Additionally, staying vigilant against cryptocurrency investment scams is crucial to safeguarding investments.

Adopting a proactive and informed approach to risk management helps minimise losses and maximises the potential for profitable outcomes. As the cryptocurrency market evolves, the principles and strategies discussed in this chapter will serve as a foundational toolkit for investors, empowering them to make more confident and strategic decisions in their investment journey.

Questions & Answers

Q Why is risk management important in cryptocurrency investments?

  A Risk management is crucial in cryptocurrency investments to protect capital, minimise losses, and optimise investment outcomes in the volatile market.

Q How can setting stop-loss orders help investors manage risk in cryptocurrency trading?

  A Stop-loss orders allow investors to automatically sell assets at predetermined prices, helping limit potential losses and protect investments during market fluctuations.

Q What role does leverage management play in risk management strategies for cryptocurrency investors?

  A Effective leverage management helps investors control their exposure to market risks, avoid excessive losses, and make informed trading decisions.

Q How does diversification across asset classes contribute to risk management in cryptocurrency investments?

  A Diversifying across different assets helps spread risk, reduce exposure to market volatility, and protect the overall portfolio from significant losses.

Q Why are case studies in risk management valuable for cryptocurrency investors?

  A Case studies provide real-world examples of risk management strategies in action, offering insights into successful approaches and highlighting the importance of managing risks effectively.

Chapter 8

Market Analysis Techniques for Cryptocurrency Investors

Technical Analysis Indicators

Technical analysis is a fundamental tool for cryptocurrency investors to interpret market data and predict future price movements. Common indicators such as moving averages, the Relative Strength Index (RSI), Bollinger Bands, and the Stochastic Oscillator play crucial roles in this analysis.

Moving averages smooth out price data to create a single flowing line, making it easier to identify the direction of the trend.

The RSI measures the speed and change of price movements to determine overbought or oversold conditions.

Bollinger Bands provide a relative view of high and low prices, which can help investors identify when an asset is trading outside its typical range and, thus, likely to revert.

The Stochastic Oscillator is another momentum indicator that compares a particular closing price of an asset to a range of its prices over a certain period, helping to identify potential reversal points by signalling overbought or oversold conditions.

By utilising these indicators, investors can make more informed decisions by analysing price trends and market momentum.

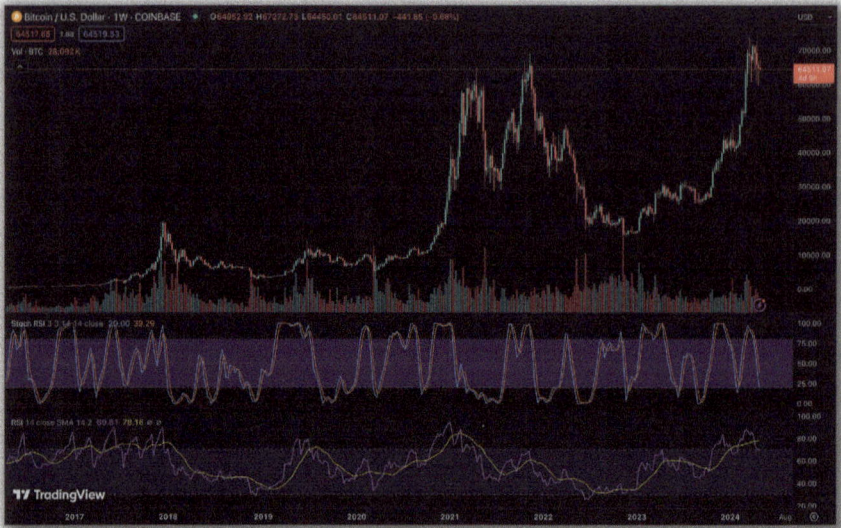

Source: TradingView

Fundamental Analysis Factors

In cryptocurrency investing, fundamental analysis involves evaluating the intrinsic value of a digital asset by analysing related economic, financial, and other qualitative and quantitative factors.

Key elements include scrutinising project whitepapers, the development team's expertise, strategic partnerships, and user adoption rates. A robust whitepaper can give investors confidence in the project's viability and innovation, while a knowledgeable team ensures effective execution.

Partnerships with established companies can enhance credibility, and user adoption rates indicate the cryptocurrency's growing acceptance and usability.

These factors collectively help investors assess a cryptocurrency's long-term potential and stability.

Sentiment Analysis Tools

Sentiment analysis tools are increasingly vital in cryptocurrency markets, where investor sentiment can significantly influence price movements. These tools analyse vast amounts of data from social media platforms, news articles, and market trends to gauge the market's mood.

Investors can anticipate potential price movements and make more informed decisions by understanding whether the sentiment is predominantly positive, negative, or neutral. This type of analysis is beneficial in the highly volatile crypto market, where public perception can drastically affect the market's direction.

Cryptocurrency Market Volatility

Cryptocurrency market volatility refers to the rapid and unpredictable price swings in digital asset markets. Factors driving this volatility include technological advancements, regulatory news, market sentiment, and macroeconomic events. High volatility in cryptocurrencies can offer investors both opportunities and risks.

Investors should use risk management strategies, such as setting stop-loss orders, diversifying their portfolios, and staying informed about market trends to manage and capitalise on market volatility. Technical and fundamental analysis tools can help investors predict price movements and make informed trading decisions.

Understanding the dynamics of cryptocurrency market volatility is crucial for investors to navigate the market effectively and make strategic investment choices.

Practical Application of Market Analysis

The practical application of market analysis in cryptocurrency investing involves a combination of technical, fundamental, and sentiment analyses to form a comprehensive view of the market. For instance, an investor might use technical analysis to determine the correct entry and exit points and complement this with fundamental analysis to select cryptocurrencies with solid potential for growth and stability.

Sentiment analysis could then be used to time these trades based on current investor mood and market trends. This holistic approach allows investors to react to the market conditions and anticipate changes, thereby maximising potential returns and minimising risks.

Case Studies in Market Analysis

Case studies often demonstrate the successful application of market analysis techniques in the cryptocurrency field. For example, an investor who analysed Bitcoin's historical price data using technical indicators like MACD and RSI could have predicted the 2017 and 2020 bull runs. Similarly, fundamental analysis of Ethereum's development progress and adoption could have informed investors about its potential prior to the major updates that led to price increases.

Another case is using sentiment analysis tools to capitalise on rapid shifts in market sentiment during high-impact events like regulatory announcements or technological breakthroughs. These case studies highlight how different market analysis techniques can effectively identify investment opportunities and manage risks in the dynamic cryptocurrency market.

Conclusion

Through these techniques, cryptocurrency investors can better understand market dynamics and improve their ability to make strategic investment decisions in a highly unpredictable environment.

Questions & Answers

Q What are technical analysis indicators, and how do they help cryptocurrency investors?

A Technical analysis indicators are tools used to analyse price movements and trends in the market, aiding investors in making informed trading decisions based on historical data.

Q How do fundamental analysis factors contribute to evaluating cryptocurrencies for investment?

A Fundamental analysis factors focus on the intrinsic value and potential growth of cryptocurrencies, considering aspects like technology, team, adoption, and market demand.

Q What role do sentiment analysis tools play in cryptocurrency market analysis?

A Sentiment analysis tools help investors gauge market sentiment, investor emotions, and social media trends to assess market sentiment and potential price movements.

Q How can investors practically apply market analysis techniques in cryptocurrency trading?

A Practical application involves using a combination of technical, fundamental, and sentiment analysis to make informed decisions, identify trends, and manage risks effectively.

Q Why are case studies in market analysis important for cryptocurrency investors?

A Case studies provide practical examples of how market analysis techniques can be applied, showcasing successful strategies and highlighting the impact of analysis on investment decisions.

Chapter 9

Choosing the Right Cryptocurrencies

Identifying Leading Cryptocurrencies

Research extensively to identify cryptocurrencies with solid fundamentals. Utilise resources like CoinMarketCap and CoinGecko to research cryptocurrencies. Look beyond the hype by analysing:

1. **Market Capitalisation:** Reflects the cryptocurrency's market value and growth potential.

2. **Daily Traded Volumes:** Indicates liquidity and investor interest.

3. **Number of Markets (Exchanges):** Assess the ease of trading and the legitimacy of platforms based on their KYC processes and establishment duration. Availability on major exchanges indicates broader acceptance and liquidity.

4. **Blockchain Foundation:** When choosing a cryptocurrency, opting for well-established blockchains might be a safer choice in terms of security and widespread usage. Proprietary blockchains may have undiscovered flaws and risks that pose a threat. However, it is essential to note that some of the best cryptocurrencies we know today were once launched as new technology. That being said, exercising caution when investing in new altcoins is always advisable, as the risks involved are higher. Nevertheless, investing in new altcoins could lead to significant returns if they turn out to be successful.

5. **Trading Pairs Availability:** Having more trading pairs for cryptocurrencies on various exchanges offers several benefits that enhance both the accessibility and liquidity of those cryptocurrencies. Here are key reasons why it is advantageous:

- **Increased Accessibility**: More trading pairs mean that investors and traders can directly exchange a cryptocurrency with a wider variety of other cryptocurrencies or fiat currencies without needing to first convert to a more common currency like Bitcoin (BTC) or Ethereum (ETH). This direct access can save on transaction fees and time.

- **Enhanced Liquidity**: Liquidity refers to how easily and quickly a cryptocurrency can be bought or sold in the market without affecting its price. A higher number of trading pairs usually correlates with higher liquidity, making it easier for traders to enter or exit positions. This is particularly beneficial during volatile market conditions.

- **Market Depth**: With more trading pairs, there is typically more market depth, meaning more buy and sell orders at various price levels. This can lead to more stable prices and less slippage (the difference between the expected price of a trade and the price at which the trade is executed).

- **Arbitrage Opportunities**: More trading pairs across different exchanges can lead to price discrepancies for the same cryptocurrency between those exchanges. Savvy traders can exploit these differences through arbitrage, buying low on one exchange and selling high on another, thus profiting from the price gap.

- **Diversification**: For investors looking to diversify their portfolio, having a variety of trading pairs allows for easier swapping between different asset classes (e.g., from cryptocurrencies to stablecoins or fiat currencies) without the need to cash out to a bank account.

- **Global Reach and Adoption**: Exchanges in different regions may prioritise trading pairs that cater to local preferences and fiat currencies. More trading pairs mean a cryptocurrency is more globally accessible, potentially increasing its user base and adoption rate.

- **Reduced Dependency on Major Cryptocurrencies**: While Bitcoin and Ethereum are the most common base currencies for trading pairs, their dominance can introduce systemic risks if there are issues with either of those blockchains. More trading pairs with a variety of cryptocurrencies reduce this dependency and potential risk.

In summary, more trading pairs for cryptocurrencies enhance the overall ecosystem by providing better liquidity, accessibility, and opportunities for traders and investors, contributing to the health and growth of the cryptocurrency market.

6. **Development Team:** A strong, active development team suggests ongoing improvements and sustainability.

7. **News History and Price Chart Analysis:** To make wise investment decisions, it's essential to keep an eye on the market's ups and downs and analyse past trends. By doing so, investors can identify volatility patterns and adjust their approach to reduce risk. Therefore, it's crucial to stay aware of market fluctuations and study historical data to make informed investment choices.

Industry Insights and Trends for Informed Cryptocurrency Investing

Analysing industry data and trends is essential for cryptocurrency investors to make informed decisions. Understanding the amounts and ratios between different coins and jurisdictions provides insights into market dynamics and investment opportunities.

For example, analysing trading volumes and market capitalisation can help investors identify trends and emerging cryptocurrencies with growth potential. Investors can also track the performance of various coins across different jurisdictions to assess market sentiment and regulatory developments. By staying informed about industry data and trends, investors can adapt their investment strategies to capitalise on market opportunities and mitigate risks effectively.

Conclusion

Investors who want to choose the right cryptocurrencies need to conduct thorough research and analysis. By focusing on cryptocurrencies with strong fundamentals, market acceptance, and growth potential, investors can increase their chances of successful investments.

It is important to evaluate market capitalisation and daily traded volumes to gain valuable insights into the liquidity and growth potential of different digital assets. By going beyond surface-level information and delving into the core aspects of leading cryptocurrencies, investors can strategically position themselves in the dynamic crypto market, aligning their investments with their financial goals and risk tolerance.

Questions & Answers

Q Why is identifying leading cryptocurrencies important for investors?

    A Identifying leading cryptocurrencies helps investors focus on assets with strong fundamentals, market acceptance, and growth potential, enhancing the likelihood of successful investments.

Q What are the industry insights and trends that inform cryptocurrency investing decisions?

    A Industry insights and trends provide valuable information on market dynamics, emerging technologies, regulatory changes, and investor sentiment, helping investors make informed decisions in the cryptocurrency space.

Chapter 10

Understanding Crypto Indexes

In the ever-changing world of cryptocurrency investing, it's crucial to understand the role of crypto indexes in making informed investment decisions and maximising portfolio performance. This section explores the importance of crypto indexes, how they are constructed, and their strategic implications for investors.

Introduction to Crypto Indexes

Crypto indexes act as benchmarks that monitor the performance of a particular group of cryptocurrencies. By representing the overall performance of the cryptocurrency market or specific sectors within it, they offer investors a comprehensive view of the market.

Types of Crypto Indexes

1. **Market Cap Weighted Indexes**: These indexes are weighted based on the market capitalisation of individual cryptocurrencies, giving higher weight to assets with larger market caps.

2. **Price-Weighted Indexes**: Price-weighted indexes assign weights based on the price of each cryptocurrency. Higher-priced assets have a more significant impact on the index value.

3. **Equal-Weighted Indexes**: Equal-weighted indexes allocate the same weight to each cryptocurrency in the index, regardless of market capitalisation or price.

Construction Methodologies

Crypto indexes are constructed using predefined methodologies to ensure accuracy and representativeness. Common methodologies include:

- **Top N Index**: Includes the top N cryptocurrencies by market capitalisation.

- **Sector-Specific Index**: Focuses on a specific sector within the cryptocurrency market, such as DeFi or privacy coins.

- **Rule-Based Index**: Follows specific rules for including and excluding cryptocurrencies based on predefined criteria.

CoinDesk 20 Index (CD20)

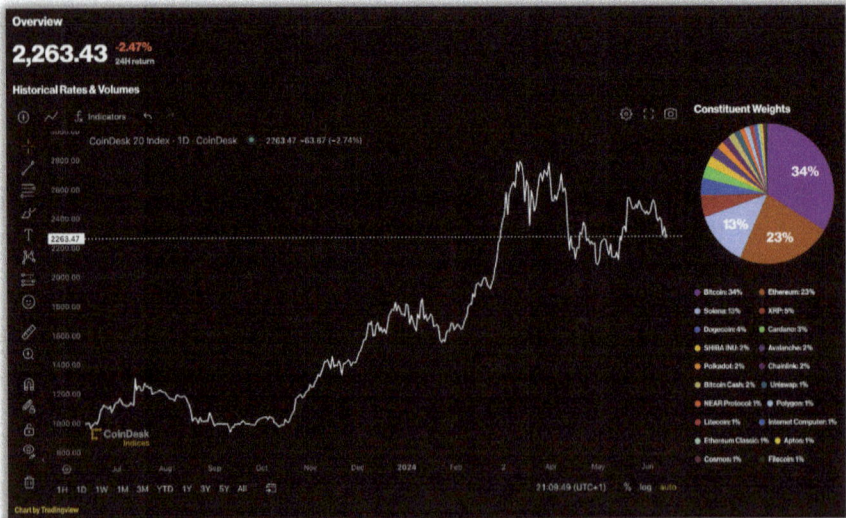

Source: *https://www.coindesk.com/indices/cd20*

Strategic Implications for Investors

1. **Diversification**: Investing in crypto indexes provides broad market exposure and diversification, reducing the risk associated with individual asset selection.

2. **Performance Evaluation**: Crypto indexes function as performance benchmarks, allowing investors to evaluate their portfolios against the overall market.

3. **Investment Opportunities**: Understanding cryptocurrency indexes can help investors spot emerging trends and investment opportunities within the crypto market.

Implementation in Investment Strategies

- **Index Funds**: Investors can access crypto indexes through index funds, which mirror the performance of the underlying index.

- **ETFs**: Exchange-traded funds (ETFs) based on cryptocurrency indexes offer investors a convenient way to gain diversified exposure to the cryptocurrency market.

Conclusion

By understanding the role of cryptocurrency indexes in the crypto ecosystem, investors can utilise these tools to improve their investment strategies, minimise risks, and take advantage of market opportunities.

Questions & Answers

Q How are crypto indexes constructed, and what are the common methodologies used?

> ***A*** Crypto indexes are constructed using methodologies such as market cap weighting, price weighting, and equal weighting to represent the performance of the cryptocurrency market.

Q How can investors benefit from investing in crypto indexes?

> ***A*** Investing in crypto indexes allows for diversification, performance evaluation, and identification of investment opportunities within the cryptocurrency market.

Q What are the strategic implications of understanding crypto indexes for investors?

> ***A*** Strategic implications include diversification, performance evaluation, and the ability to capitalise on market trends and opportunities.

Q How can investors implement crypto indexes in their investment strategies?

> ***A*** Investors can access crypto indexes through index funds and ETFs, providing diversified exposure to the cryptocurrency market.

Q What are crypto indexes, and why are they important for investors?

> ***A*** Crypto indexes are tools that track the performance of a group of cryptocurrencies, providing investors with a benchmark to measure overall market performance and make informed investment decisions.

Chapter 11

Introduction to Short-Selling Cryptocurrencies

Short-selling is an advanced trading strategy that enables investors to profit from falling prices in the cryptocurrency market. In contrast to traditional "long" positions, where investors purchase assets in the hope that their value will increase, Short-selling involves borrowing assets to sell at the current price and buying them back later at a lower price. This section will explore the mechanics, strategies, benefits, and risks of short-selling cryptocurrencies.

Mechanics of Short-Selling Cryptocurrencies

Short-selling cryptocurrency involves several steps:

1. **Borrowing the Asset**: Begin by borrowing the cryptocurrency an investor wants to short from a reputable exchange or broker that offers margin trading. The exchange lends the asset, often charging interest for the loan.

   Example: An investor believes Bitcoin's price will fall from its current $60,000. They borrow 10 BTC from their exchange.

2. **Selling the Borrowed Asset**: After borrowing the asset, the investor sells it immediately at the current market price.

   Example: The investor sells the borrowed 10 BTC for $60,000 each.

3. **Waiting for the Price to Fall**: Next, the investor waits for the price to decrease. If the prediction is correct, the asset's value will decline.

   Example: Over the next week, Bitcoin's price falls to $54,000.

4. **Buying Back and Returning the Asset**: When the investor believes the price has fallen sufficiently, or if there is a need to minimise losses, they buy back the same amount of the asset at the new, lower cost and return it to the lender.

   Example: The investor buys back 10 BTC at $54,000 each and returns it to the exchange.

5. **Profit Calculation**: The profit (or loss) is the difference between the selling and buying prices minus any fees or interest charged by the exchange.

   Example: Profit = (60,000 * 10BTC) − (54,000 * 10 BTC) = $60,000 (minus fees and interest).

Strategies for Short-Selling Cryptocurrencies

- **Technical Analysis-Based Shorting**: Use technical indicators such as moving averages, RSI, Stochastic, or MACD to identify potential downtrends.

  Example: An investor notices that Ethereum has broken below its 50-day moving average and decides to open a short position.

- **News-Driven Shorting**: React to negative news or events that could impact a cryptocurrency's price.

  Example: Following news of a major hack on a popular DeFi platform, an investor shorts the associated token, anticipating a price drop.

- **Overvaluation Shorting**: Short assets that appear overvalued based on fundamental analysis.

Example: An investor believes a newly launched "meme coin" is significantly overvalued and opens a short position, expecting a correction.

- **Trend Following**: Short cryptocurrencies that are already in a clear downtrend.

  Example: Bitcoin has been declining for several weeks. An investor opens a short position to capitalise on the continuing downtrend.

- **Pairs Trading**: Simultaneously go long on one cryptocurrency and short another, betting on the relative performance between the two.

  Example: An investor goes long on Bitcoin and shorts a smaller altcoin, expecting Bitcoin to outperform.

Benefits of Short-Selling Cryptocurrencies

- **Profit Potential in Bear Markets**: Short-selling cryptocurrencies offers a unique opportunity to make profits even when the market is down, presenting a potential silver lining in times of negative sentiment.

- **Portfolio Hedging**: Short positions can protect long-term holdings and minimise potential losses.

- **Market Efficiency**: Short-selling can help correct overvalued assets, contributing to more efficient price discovery in the market.

- **Diversification**: Incorporating short positions into a portfolio can effectively diversify and potentially reduce overall portfolio risk, providing a sense of security and control.

Considerations & Risks of Short-Selling Cryptocurrencies

- **Unlimited Loss Potential**: Unlike long positions, where losses are limited to the initial investment, short positions have theoretically unlimited loss potential if the asset's price increases indefinitely.

  Example: An investor shorts Bitcoin at $60,000. If Bitcoin's price rises to $120,000, the investor would incur a loss equivalent to 100% of their initial position size.

- **Margin Calls**: Short-selling typically involves margin trading. If the trade moves against the investor, they may face margin calls requiring additional funds to keep the position open.

  Example: An investor shorts Ethereum with 5x leverage. If Ethereum's price increases by 20%, they may receive a margin call.

- **Short Squeezes**: A rapid increase in an asset's price can force short-sellers to buy back the asset to cover their positions, further driving up the price.

  Example: The GameStop short squeeze in traditional markets demonstrated how coordinated buying can dramatically increase prices, causing significant losses for short-sellers.

- **Borrowing Costs**: Exchanges charge interest on borrowed assets, which can eat into profits, especially for long-term short positions.

  Example: An exchange charges 0.1% daily interest on borrowed Bitcoin. For a 30-day short position, this amounts to 3% of the position size.

- **Regulatory Risks**: Short-selling regulations in the cryptocurrency market are evolving and can vary by jurisdiction. Changes in regulations could impact the ability to short-sell or increase associated costs.

Practical Steps for Short-Selling Cryptocurrencies

- **Choose a Reliable Exchange**: Select a reputable cryptocurrency exchange with margin trading and short-selling capabilities. Examples include Binance, BitMEX, and Kraken.

- **Understand the Platform's Rules**: Investors must familiarise themselves with the exchange's policies on margin requirements, liquidation procedures, and borrowing costs. This knowledge will keep them informed and prepared for any situation.

- **Start Small**: For beginners, it's advisable to begin with small positions to gain experience and understand the mechanics of short-selling without risking significant capital. This prudent approach can help build confidence and skills in short-selling.

- **Use Stop-Loss Orders**: Implement stop-loss orders to limit potential losses if the trade moves against the investor. For example, when shorting Bitcoin at $60,000, set a stop-loss at $63,000 to limit potential losses to 5% of the position size.

- **Monitor Positions**: Regularly check open positions and be prepared to act quickly if market conditions change.

- **Manage Risk**: A fundamental principle of trading is to never risk more than what can be afforded to lose. When short-selling, it's important to consider using only a small portion of the overall portfolio and to always manage risk effectively.

Case Study: Successful Short-Selling Strategy

In early 2022, an experienced cryptocurrency trader observed that the Terra/LUNA ecosystem exhibited signs of instability despite its high valuation. The trader pinpointed potential flaws in the algorithmic stablecoin model.

Strategy: The trader opened a short position on LUNA while trading at $80. They set a stop-loss at $88 to limit potential losses. As concerns about Terra's stability grew, LUNA's price began to fall. The trader gradually increased their short position as the price declined, carefully managing their risk exposure. When LUNA's price collapsed to near zero, the trader closed their position, realising significant profits.

Key Takeaways:

1. Thorough research and understanding of the underlying technology were crucial.

2. Risk management through careful position sizing and stop-loss orders was essential.

3. The trader remained flexible, adjusting their strategy as the market situation evolved.

Conclusion

Short-selling cryptocurrencies can be a powerful tool for experienced traders, offering opportunities to profit in various market conditions and enhance overall portfolio management. However, it comes with significant risks and requires careful planning, execution, and ongoing management. As with all trading strategies, thorough research, risk management, and a deep understanding of market dynamics are essential for success in short-selling cryptocurrencies.

Questions & Answers

Q What is short-selling in the context of cryptocurrency investing?

    A Short-selling is an advanced trading strategy where investors profit from falling prices by borrowing assets, selling them at the current price, and buying them back later at a lower price.

Q What are the key steps involved in short-selling cryptocurrencies?

    A The key steps are: 1) Borrowing the asset from an exchange, 2) Selling the borrowed asset at the current market price, 3) Waiting for the price to fall, 4) Buying back the asset at a lower price, and 5) Returning the borrowed asset to the lender.

Q What are some strategies for short-selling cryptocurrencies?

    A Some strategies include trend following, news-based trading, technical analysis, and pairs trading.

Q What are the potential benefits of short-selling cryptocurrencies?

    A Benefits include profit potential in bear markets, portfolio hedging, and increased market liquidity.

Q What are the main risks associated with short-selling cryptocurrencies?

    A The main risks include potentially unlimited losses, margin calls, high borrowing costs, and regulatory risks.

Q How can investors mitigate risks when short-selling cryptocurrencies?

    A Risk mitigation strategies include thorough research, setting stop-loss orders, practising with small positions, and staying informed about market conditions and regulations.

Chapter 12

Decentralised Finance (DeFi) vs. Centralised Exchanges for Trading

Decentralised finance (DeFi) platforms and centralised exchanges represent two fundamentally different approaches to cryptocurrency trading, each with unique advantages and challenges. Understanding these differences is crucial for making informed decisions when entering the crypto space.

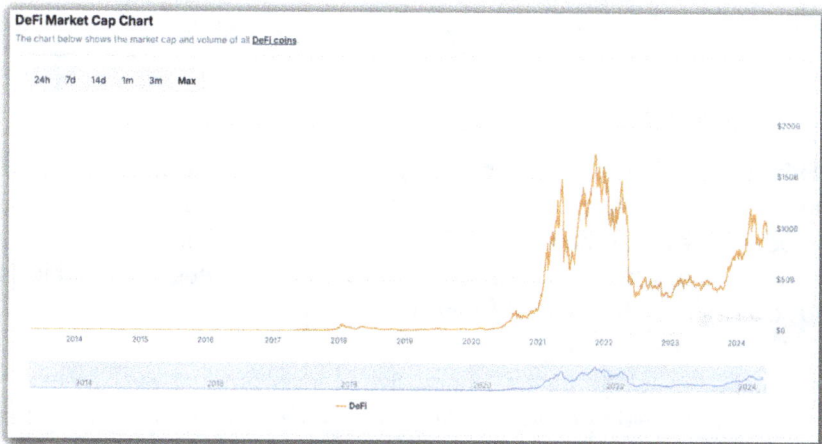

DeFi coins market cap and volume. Source: CoinGecko

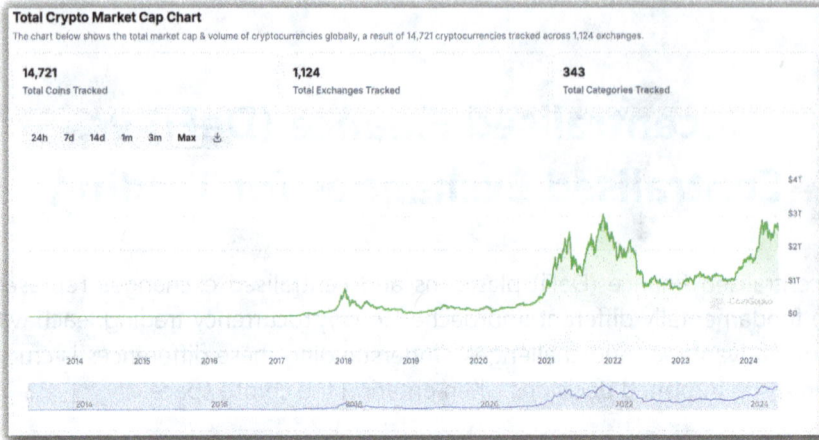

Total Crypto Market Cap Chart
The chart below shows the total market cap & volume of cryptocurrencies globally, a result of 14,721 cryptocurrencies tracked across 1,124 exchanges.

14,721	1,124	343
Total Coins Tracked	Total Exchanges Tracked	Total Categories Tracked

24h   7d   14d   1m   3m   Max

Total market cap and volume. Source: CoinGecko

Control and Ownership

DeFi Platforms: DeFi platforms provide users with complete control over their funds. Unlike centralised exchanges, where users deposit their cryptocurrencies into the exchange's custodial wallets, DeFi platforms allow users to trade directly from their own wallets. This eliminates the risk of losing funds due to an exchange hack or insolvency.

Additionally, DeFi platforms offer innovative financial products such as lending, borrowing, and yield farming, enabling users to earn passive income on their crypto assets.

However, using DeFi platforms requires a higher level of technical expertise. Users must understand how to interact with smart contracts and navigate the often complex interfaces of DeFi applications. This complexity can be a significant barrier for beginners.

Centralised Exchanges: On the other hand, centralised exchanges offer a more user-friendly experience. These platforms typically feature intuitive interfaces and customer support, making them more accessible to beginners. Users can trade various cryptocurrencies and often benefit from higher liquidity, making it easier to execute large trades without significantly impacting the market price.

Asset Types and Fiat Integration

DeFi Platforms: DeFi platforms typically only support the exchange of cryptocurrencies. They do not directly integrate with fiat currencies such as USD or EUR. Those interested in participating in DeFi first need to obtain stablecoins (e.g., USDT, USDC, DAI) or other cryptocurrencies through centralised exchanges or other methods. This two-step process can be burdensome and involves additional risks and fees.

Centralised Exchanges: These platforms generally facilitate fiat-to-crypto transactions, enabling users to deposit fiat currencies and directly convert them into cryptocurrencies. This simplifies the process for most users, eliminating the need for intermediary steps and reducing transaction complexity.

Security Concerns

DeFi Platforms: Security remains a significant concern in the DeFi space. While the decentralised nature of these platforms reduces the risk of a single point of failure, it does not eliminate risk altogether. Hackers can exploit smart contract vulnerabilities, leading to significant financial losses. Additionally, newer projects may not be as rigorously audited, increasing the risk of bugs and vulnerabilities.

Centralised Exchanges: While centralised exchanges can implement stringent security measures, they are still attractive targets for hackers due to the large volumes of assets they hold. Security breaches can result in the loss of user funds, as has happened with several high-profile exchange hacks. Regulatory scrutiny and compliance are also critical factors, as exchanges operating without proper licenses may face shutdowns or legal challenges.

Complexity and Usability

DeFi Platforms: DeFi platforms can be quite complex, especially for beginners. Users need to grasp how to use digital wallets, engage with different DeFi applications, and handle private keys. The interfaces of DeFi platforms often assume a certain level of familiarity with blockchain technology, which can deter less tech-savvy investors from getting involved.

Centralised Exchanges: Centralised exchanges are more user-friendly, making them a more attractive option for new investors. These platforms offer a seamless experience with features such as customer support, easy-to-navigate interfaces, and educational resources to help users understand the trading process. This ease of use can significantly reduce the barrier to entry for cryptocurrency trading.

Liquidity

DeFi Platforms: One area where DeFi platforms can fall behind their centralised counterparts is liquidity. Despite substantial growth in recent years, decentralised platforms often have less liquidity compared to major centralised exchanges. This can lead to higher slippage and less efficient trading, especially for large orders.

Centralised Exchanges: Centralised exchanges generally provide higher liquidity due to their large user bases and the consolidation of market activity. This increased liquidity makes it easier to execute large trades without significantly impacting the market price.

Investor Considerations

When choosing between DeFi platforms and centralised exchanges, investors should consider several factors:

- **Security**: Evaluate the security measures and past track records of the platforms.

- **Liquidity**: Determine the liquidity needs and choose a platform that can accommodate larger trades efficiently if necessary.

- **Regulatory Compliance**: Consider the regulatory environment and ensure the platform operates within legal frameworks.

- **Ease of Use**: Assess the technical expertise required to use the platforms and choose accordingly based on comfort and familiarity with crypto technologies.

- **Access to Fiat**: Decide whether direct conversion between fiat and crypto is essential, which may necessitate the use of centralised exchanges.

- **Innovative Products**: DeFi platforms offer more opportunities for advanced financial products like lending or yield farming.

Conclusion

It's important for cryptocurrency investors to understand the differences between decentralised finance (DeFi) platforms and centralised exchanges. DeFi platforms give users full control over their funds and offer innovative financial products and passive income opportunities. However, they require more technical expertise and may have lower liquidity compared to centralised exchanges.

On the other hand, centralised exchanges are easier to use, offer higher liquidity, and allow for fiat integration, making them more accessible to beginners. When choosing between DeFi platforms and centralised exchanges, investors should consider security, complexity, usability, and liquidity.

By evaluating these factors and aligning them with their individual risk tolerance and investment goals, investors can make informed decisions in the cryptocurrency trading landscape.

Questions & Answers

Q What are the key considerations for investors when choosing between decentralised finance (DeFi) platforms and centralised exchanges?

   A Investors should evaluate factors such as security, asset control, liquidity, complexity, usability, and fiat integration when deciding between DeFi platforms and centralised exchanges.

Q How do DeFi platforms differ from centralised exchanges in terms of user control and financial products?

   A DeFi platforms offer users complete control over their funds and access to innovative financial products, while centralised exchanges provide a user-friendly experience and higher liquidity.

Q Why is it important for investors to assess security concerns when selecting between DeFi platforms and centralised exchanges?

   A Evaluating security measures is crucial to safeguarding assets and mitigating risks associated with trading on DeFi platforms or centralised exchanges.

Chapter 13

Case Studies on Successful Investments in Cryptocurrency

The cryptocurrency market has seen many success stories where investors have achieved remarkable returns. These offer practical lessons for both new and seasoned investors. Here are some examples:

Early Bitcoin Investors

One of the most well-known success stories in cryptocurrency investment involves the early adopters of Bitcoin.

For example, an individual who bought Bitcoin when it was priced at less than $1 in 2009 and held onto it until it reached its peak (surpassing $70,000 in 2024) would have experienced an enormous return on investment.

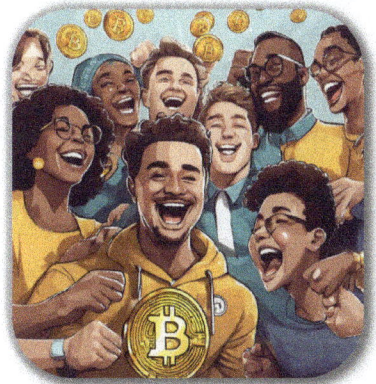

This case highlights the potential of long-term holding in appreciating the value of cryptocurrencies and the importance of early recognition and investing in innovative technologies.

Ethereum's Initial Coin Offering (ICO)

Investors participating in Ethereum's ICO in 2014 bought Ether for around $0.30 to $0.40 per coin. Since then, Ethereum has developed into a foundational blockchain platform that supports various applications, including smart contracts and decentralised applications (DApps). As a result, the value of Ether has surged and reached a high of over $4,500 in 2021.

This case study highlights the potential for high investment returns in ICOs while emphasising the importance of understanding the underlying technology and the development team's capabilities.

Binance Coin (BNB)

Binance Coin (BNB) was introduced in 2017 as a utility token for the Binance cryptocurrency exchange. During its initial coin offering (ICO), each token was priced at around $0.10. Since then, Binance has grown significantly and expanded its services beyond a trading platform. As a result, the value of BNB has also increased.

BNB is used to pay transaction fees on the Binance exchange, participate in token sales, and more.

Diversifying BNB's use cases has helped boost its value, demonstrating the importance of utility and real-world application when considering cryptocurrency investments.

The Link Marine Community and Chainlink

Chainlink (LINK) is an excellent example of how a cryptocurrency can succeed through community-driven investment. Its primary function is to facilitate data transfer between external data sources and smart contracts on the blockchain.

The project gained massive attention and investment from a dedicated community known as "Link Marine."

As Chainlink continued to secure partnerships and integrations across various industries, LINK's value saw significant growth. Investors who recognised the potential of decentralised oracle networks and invested in LINK benefited greatly as the token's value increased multiple times.

This case highlights the crucial role of community support and strategic partnerships in driving the success of a cryptocurrency.

Solana's Rapid Ascent

Solana's blockchain platform has gained significant attention due to its high throughput and low transaction costs, which have addressed some scalability issues that earlier blockchains like Ethereum face.

Investors who recognised the potential of Solana's technology in supporting scalable DApps and invested early have witnessed considerable returns, particularly during its peak periods in 2021. This example highlights the importance of technological innovation and market positioning in selecting investment opportunities.

Conclusion

These case studies demonstrate various factors that can lead to successful investments in the cryptocurrency market, including the timing of the investment, the technological foundation of the asset, the utility and real-world application of the token, and the strength of the community and partnerships. Each story offers valuable lessons on strategic investment and the potential for high returns while also cautioning about the volatility and risks inherent in the cryptocurrency market.

Questions & Answers

Q What can we learn from early Bitcoin investors in the cryptocurrency market?

    A Early Bitcoin investors demonstrate the potential for significant returns by holding onto assets through market fluctuations and showcasing the long-term growth potential of cryptocurrencies.

Q How did Ethereum's Initial Coin Offering (ICO) impact the cryptocurrency market?

    A Ethereum's ICO revolutionised fundraising in the blockchain space, showcasing the potential for crowdfunding projects and driving innovation in smart contracts and decentralised applications.

Q What makes Binance Coin (BNB) a successful investment case study in the cryptocurrency market?

    A Binance Coin's success is attributed to its utility within the Binance ecosystem, offering discounts on trading fees and incentives for users, leading to increased adoption and value appreciation.

Q What role did The Link Marine Community play in the success of Chainlink in the cryptocurrency market?

    A The Link Marine Community actively supported Chainlink's development, adoption, and community engagement, contributing to its growth and success as a decentralised oracle network.

Q How did Solana experience rapid ascent in the cryptocurrency market?

    A Solana's rapid ascent can be attributed to its high-performance blockchain technology, scalability, and developer-friendly ecosystem, positioning it as a leading platform for decentralised applications and smart contracts.

Chapter 14

Analysis and Advanced Trading Strategies

Cryptocurrency trading demands a robust understanding of technical analysis and the sophisticated trading tools available on various exchanges. This comprehensive guide delves into the essential technical indicators and analysis tools alongside advanced trading options and environments provided by major cryptocurrency exchanges, focusing on how these resources can enhance trading strategies and risk management.

Technical Analysis: Essential Tools and Indicators

Technical analysis (TA) is a methodology for forecasting the direction of prices through the study of past market data, primarily price and volume. It is widely used in cryptocurrency trading to predict future market behaviour based on historical patterns. This section explores various technical analysis tools, explains their significance, how to combine them effectively, and discusses considerations for their use, including correlations with other financial instruments.

1. **Candlestick Charts**: These charts are fundamental to TA and provide visual insights into market psychology. Each candlestick displays the open, high, low, and close prices for a specific period. Patterns within these charts can indicate potential market reversals or continuation of trends.

2. **Moving Averages (SMA and EMA)**: These include Simple Moving Averages (SMA) and Exponential Moving Averages (EMA). MAs

smooth out price data to identify the trend direction. The SMA gives equal weighting to all values, while the EMA places more weight on recent data, making it more responsive to new information.

3. **Relative Strength Index (RSI)**: RSI measures the speed and change of price movements on a scale of 0 to 100. Generally, an RSI above 70 indicates overbought conditions, while below 30 suggests oversold conditions.

4. **MACD (Moving Average Convergence Divergence)**: This tool helps identify changes in momentum by comparing two moving averages. A MACD crossover above the signal line can indicate a bullish signal, whereas a crossover below can indicate a bearish signal.

5. **Fibonacci Retracement**: Used to identify potential reversal levels, these are horizontal lines that indicate where support and resistance are likely to occur based on past price movements and retracements.

6. **Bollinger Bands**: These bands adjust themselves to market conditions by measuring volatility. When the bands tighten, it indicates low volatility and is often considered a precursor to future volatility and potential trading opportunities.

7. **Stochastic Oscillator**: This momentum indicator compares a cryptocurrency's closing price to a range of its prices over a certain period, with sensitivity to speed and changes in price movements.

8. **Ichimoku Cloud**: A versatile indicator that provides information about support and resistance levels, momentum, and trend direction through multiple calculations, offering a comprehensive glance at possible future price action.

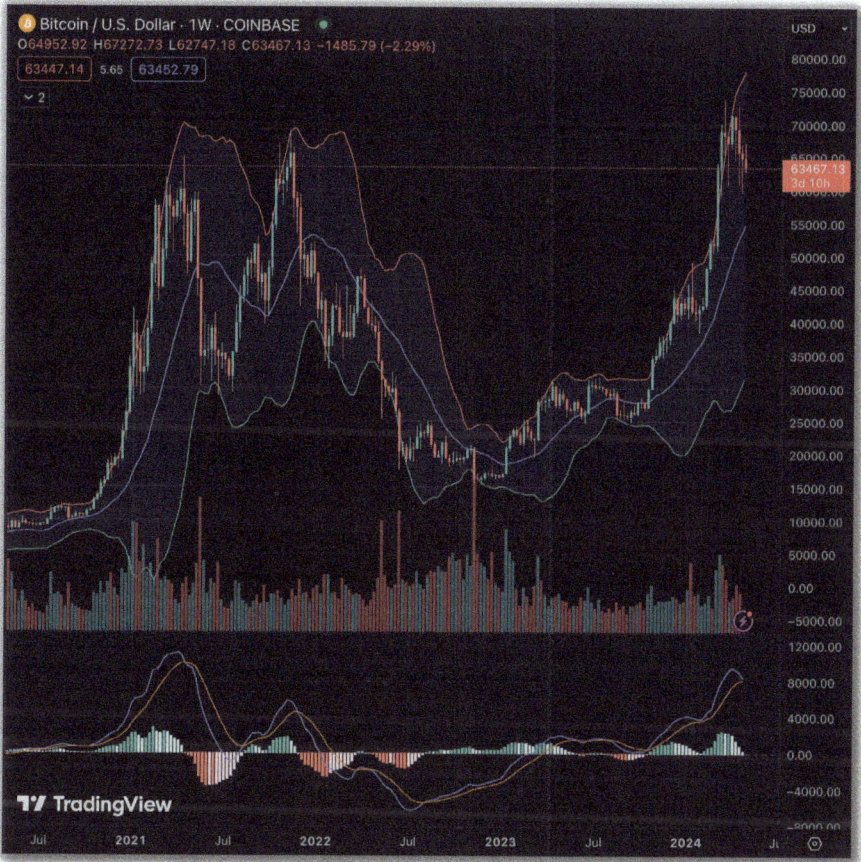

Source: TradingView

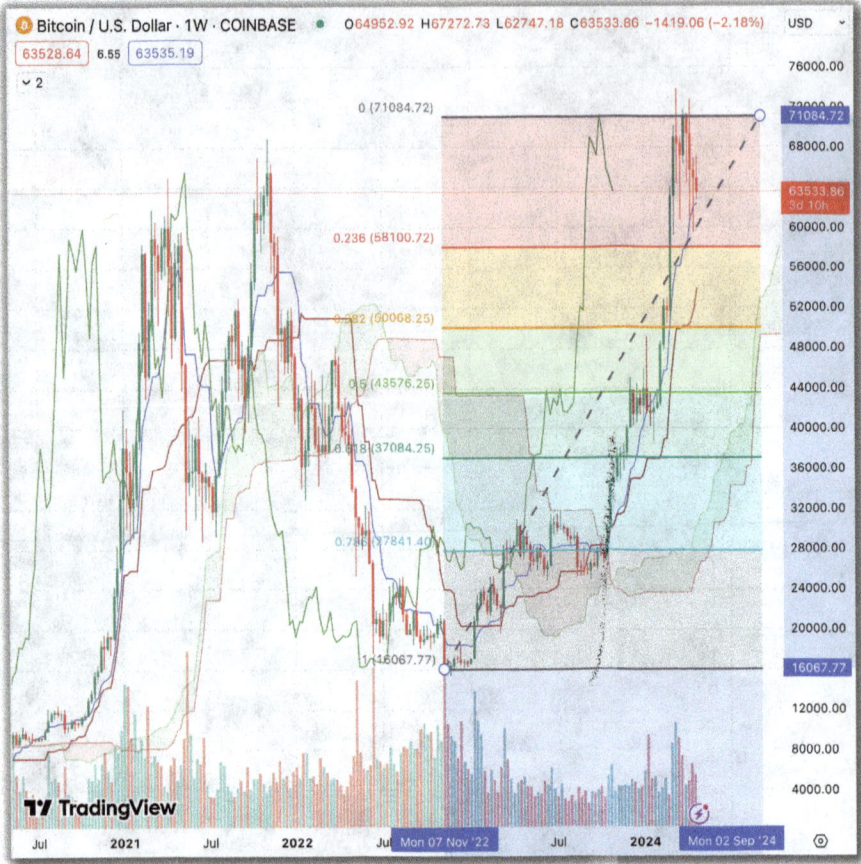

Source: TradingView

Combining Technical Analysis Tools

By combining multiple technical analysis (TA) tools, traders can generate more reliable trading signals. For instance, a trader can use the Relative Strength Index (RSI) and Moving Average Convergence Divergence (MACD) to confirm trend reversals. If RSI indicates an overbought condition and MACD shows a bearish crossover, it might suggest a strong sell signal. Similarly, moving averages with Bollinger Bands can help confirm trend directions and potential volatility.

Considerations: Historical Behaviour, Timelines, and Correlations

- **Historical Behaviour**: Analysing a cryptocurrency's past reactions can provide insights into future movements. Context is essential, as patterns often repeat themselves.

- **Timelines**: Different indicators are more suitable for different timeframes. Traders who operate over short-term periods may prefer indicators such as RSI and stochastic oscillators, while long-term investors may rely more on moving averages and MACD.

- **Correlations**: Cryptocurrencies can be correlated with other financial instruments, such as stocks, commodities, and indices. For example, Bitcoin has shown periods of correlation with traditional markets like the S&P 500, which can influence trading strategies.

- **Inter-market Analysis**: This involves analysing different but related markets to determine the strength or weakness of a cryptocurrency. For example, if tech stocks are performing well, tech-centric tokens might also see strength.

Advanced Trading Options and Environments on Cryptocurrency Exchanges

Advanced trading options and user interfaces on cryptocurrency exchanges provide the tools necessary for implementing sophisticated trading strategies:

1. **Advanced Order Types**: Stop loss, trailing stop, GTC (Good Till Cancelled), and OCO (One Cancels the Other). These tools help manage risk and are instrumental in executing complex trading strategies.

2. **Over-the-counter (OTC) Trading**: OTC trading refers to direct trades between two parties. It is preferred for large-scale investors who want to execute big trades without affecting the market price. Unlike traditional order book trading, where large orders can significantly impact the market price due to slippage, OTC trading allows for more stable pricing and better privacy.

3. **Social Trading**: By leveraging the knowledge and experience of successful traders in the community, platforms like eToro help novice traders reduce the learning curve and mimic the strategies of experts.

Benefits of OTC Trading Over Traditional Methods

OTC trading offers several advantages over traditional exchange trading:

- **Price Stability**: Large orders placed on public exchanges can cause significant price fluctuations. In contrast, OTC trades are negotiated privately and have a minimal impact on the market price.

- **Reduced Slippage**: OTC trades typically occur at a predetermined price, reducing the cost variance between an order's expected and executed price.

- **Privacy**: OTC trading offers enhanced privacy as trades are not publicly broadcasted, making it particularly beneficial for high-profile traders and institutions.

- **Customisation**: OTC deals offer flexibility, such as extended settlement periods, which can benefit large transactions.

Leading Cryptocurrency Exchanges with Advanced Features (examples)

- **Binance**: Known for its depth of market and variety of order types, including OCO and advanced technical analysis tools.

- **eToro**: Offers robust social trading features, allowing users to engage with and learn from other traders while automatically copying their trades.

- **Kraken**: Provides a suite of advanced trading options and tools, catering to both novice and experienced traders.

Conclusion

Cryptocurrency trading is a volatile market, making it essential for traders to master technical analysis and use advanced trading options. By doing so, traders can navigate the market efficiently and manage risks better.

They can also optimise their outcomes by understanding the advantages of different trading environments, such as the stability offered by OTC trading. It's important to stay informed on the latest tools and techniques to maintain a competitive edge as the market evolves.

Questions & Answers

Q **How do technical analysis tools and indicators assist cryptocurrency investors in making trading decisions?**

    A Technical analysis tools and indicators help investors analyse price movements, identify trends, and make informed trading decisions based on historical data and market patterns.

Q **What is the significance of combining technical analysis tools in cryptocurrency trading?**

    A Combining technical analysis tools enhances the accuracy of trading signals, providing investors with a more comprehensive view of market trends and potential entry and exit points.

Q **Why is considering historical behaviour, timelines, and correlations important in cryptocurrency trading?**

    A Understanding historical behaviour, timelines, and correlations helps investors predict future market movements, identify patterns, and make strategic trading decisions based on past data.

Q **How do advanced trading options and environments on cryptocurrency exchanges benefit investors?**

    A Advanced trading options on exchanges offer investors tools like stop-loss orders, trailing stops, and OCO orders, enabling them to manage risk effectively and execute complex trading strategies.

Q **What advantages does OTC trading offer over traditional methods in the cryptocurrency market?**

    A OTC trading provides more stable pricing, privacy, and the ability to execute large trades without impacting market prices significantly, making it preferable for institutional investors and high-volume traders.

Q Can you provide examples of leading cryptocurrency exchanges with advanced features?

    A Leading cryptocurrency exchanges with advanced features include Binance, Coinbase Pro, Kraken, Bitfinex, and Huobi, which offer traders a range of tools and functionalities for traders.

Chapter 15

Understanding Limit and Market Orders

Understanding the different types of orders in cryptocurrency trading is essential for executing effective trading strategies.

Two commonly used order types in trading are limit orders and market orders. Each type serves a unique purpose and comes with its own set of considerations.

Limit Orders

Definition: A limit order is buying or selling a cryptocurrency at a specific price or better. A buy limit order can only be executed at the limit price or lower, while a sell limit order can only be executed at the limit price or higher. This type of order is not guaranteed to execute.

1. **When to Use:**

   - **Precision Entry/Exit**: Limit orders should be used when one wants to enter or exit the market at a specific price.

   - **Price Control**: A limit order is appropriate if one has a target price and is willing to wait for the market to reach that price.

   - **Managing Slippage**: Limit orders help manage slippage in volatile markets by ensuring that one does not overpay or undersell.

2. **Considerations**:

   - **Partial Fills**: Limit orders may be partially filled if there is insufficient market liquidity at the desired price.

- **Missed Opportunities**: If the market does not reach the limit price, the order may not be executed, potentially causing one to miss a trading opportunity.

3. **Useful Information**:

- **Order Book Impact**: Limit orders are placed in the order book and can provide insight into potential support and resistance levels by adding liquidity to the market.

Market Orders

Definition: A market order is an order to buy or sell a cryptocurrency immediately at the best available current price. It prioritises speed over price and is typically executed within seconds.

1. **When to Use**:

- **Immediate Execution**: Market orders are used to quickly enter or exit the market with less emphasis on getting a better price.

- **High-Volatility Situations**: In highly volatile markets, when prices change rapidly, a market order ensures the execution of a trade, which can be critical for stop-loss orders.

2. **Considerations**:

- **Slippage**: Market orders can experience slippage, especially in volatile or illiquid markets, meaning the execution price may differ from the expected price.

- **Market Impact**: Large market orders can move prices, particularly in less liquid markets, potentially leading to unfavourable execution prices.

3. **Useful Information**:

- **Timing**: During periods of high trading volume, market orders offer a reduced likelihood of significant price slippage.

- **Fees**: Some exchanges charge higher fees for market orders due to the liquidity they take from the order book.

Strategic Application and Watching Points

1. **Risk Management**: It is always advisable to consider using stop-loss orders (which can be market or limit orders) to manage risks, especially in unpredictable markets.

2. **Market Conditions**: Analysing market conditions before placing an order is important. Limit orders may be more beneficial in stable, less volatile markets, while market orders may be preferable in fast-moving markets to ensure execution.

3. **Fees and Costs**: It is crucial to be aware of different fee structures on exchanges, as fees can significantly impact the profitability of one's trading strategy, especially with market and limit orders.

Conclusion

Limit and market orders are essential tools for cryptocurrency traders. Choosing between a limit and a market order depends on factors such as price certainty, execution speed, market conditions, and individual trading strategy.

Understanding the subtleties of these orders helps traders make informed decisions, manage risks effectively, and improve trading outcomes in the volatile world of cryptocurrency trading.

Questions & Answers

Q What is the purpose of limit orders in cryptocurrency trading?

   A Limit orders allow investors to buy or sell cryptocurrencies at a specific price or better, helping them control the price at which their trades are executed.

Q How do market orders function in cryptocurrency trading?

   A Market orders involve buying or selling cryptocurrencies at the current market price, ensuring immediate execution but potentially at slightly different prices than expected.

Q What are strategic applications and watching points in the context of limit and market orders?

   A The strategic application involves setting appropriate price levels for limit orders while watching points refers to monitoring market conditions to adjust orders based on price movements and trends.

Chapter 16

Security Measures, Exchanges and Wallet Management

Retaining Control and Security

- **Exchanges:** It is recommended that investors only deposit their cryptocurrencies into exchanges when they plan to trade.

  Exchanges are prone to hacks, and keeping assets on an exchange increases the risk of loss.

- **Withdraw to personal wallets:** Transfer cryptocurrencies to personal wallets for secure holding.

Choosing and Using Cryptocurrency Exchanges Safely

Cryptocurrency exchanges play a crucial role in the world of digital assets, serving as the primary venues where individuals can buy, sell, and trade cryptocurrencies. Therefore, investors need to choose a suitable exchange, as this decision can significantly impact the security and profitability of their investments.

Researching and Identifying Reputable Exchanges

Key Factors to Consider:
1. **Regulatory Compliance**: A reputable exchange adheres to regulatory requirements in its jurisdictions, which protects investors by upholding financial standards and anti-money laundering (AML) practices.

2. **Security Measures**: Investors are advised to select exchanges that implement robust security measures, such as two-factor authentication (2FA), cold storage of assets, encrypted databases, and regular security audits.

3. **Transaction Volume and Liquidity**: High trading volumes can indicate a liquid and active market, resulting in better prices and faster transaction execution.

4. **User Reviews and Community Feedback**: Researching an exchange before using it is crucial. Feedback from the community, especially from experienced traders, can provide valuable insights into the exchange's reliability and performance.

5. **Historical Performance and Incidents**: It is essential to investigate any past security breaches or technical issues that may have impacted the exchange. How the exchange handled such situations can indicate its reliability and customer service level.

Recent Notable Incidents:

- The collapse of FTX in 2023 served as a stark reminder of the potential risks associated with cryptocurrency exchanges. This event resulted in significant losses for investors and substantially impacted trust in the global crypto markets, highlighting the importance of due diligence and continuous monitoring of exchange stability and integrity.

Sources for Research:

- Websites of regulatory bodies for compliance verification.

- Crypto news websites and forums for user reviews and security breach reports.

- Financial news platforms for information on an exchange's business stability and market reputation.

Making Deposits and Withdrawals

Best Practices:

- **Verification Processes**: Completing all necessary verification processes enhances account security and increases withdrawal limits.

- **Deposit Limits**: Investors should know deposit limits and ensure they align with their investment strategy.

- **Withdrawal Policies**: Understanding the withdrawal policies, including timing, fees, and limits, is crucial. Some exchanges have restrictions that could affect investment liquidity.

- **Secure Connections**: Investors should always use a secure connection (https) when accessing their exchange accounts and avoid using public Wi-Fi for transactions.

Security Considerations

Exchange Security:

- **Cold Storage vs. Hot Wallets**: Investors are advised to opt for exchanges that keep a substantial portion of funds in cold storage, as this minimises the risk of theft through online hacks. Ideally, these exchanges should employ reputable third-party custodians with global recognition and certification.

- **Insurance Fund**: Some exchanges maintain insurance policies to cover losses from security breaches, adding an extra layer of security for investor funds.

Personal Security Practices:

- **Strong Passwords and 2FA**: Investors should use strong, unique passwords for their exchange accounts and enable two-factor authentication.

- **Regular Monitoring**: Monitoring account activity and setting up alerts for suspicious actions are essential practices.

- **Historical Hacks and Vulnerabilities**: In recent years, cryptocurrency exchanges have been subject to several significant incidents highlighting their vulnerabilities. Examples include the Mt. Gox hack in 2014, the Coincheck hack in 2018, and the FTX collapse in 2023. These events resulted in significant financial losses for investors, emphasising the importance of implementing strict security measures.

- **Regular updates are necessary to address new vulnerabilities**. Investors should remain informed about exchange security updates.

Selecting a suitable cryptocurrency exchange is a fundamental step for any investor. This requires a comprehensive evaluation of the exchange's security protocols, regulatory adherence, and operational history. Additionally, it is essential to follow best practices for account management and stay updated about potential security threats to secure investments.

By carefully choosing their trading platforms and actively managing their accounts, investors can significantly reduce the risks associated with cryptocurrency exchanges, thereby improving the security and potential success of their investment ventures.

Protecting Against Phishing Scams in Cryptocurrency Investments

In the digital investment industry, phishing is a significant threat that requires vigilance and proactive measures. Scammers use deceitful methods to trick investors into revealing sensitive information.

Phishing attacks typically involve fraudulent attempts to obtain confidential data, such as login details, private keys, or financial information, by pretending to be legitimate entities through deceptive emails, messages, or websites.

To strengthen protection against phishing attacks and improve security, investors should consider taking the following proactive measures:

- **Verify Website Authenticity**: Before entering any personal or financial details, carefully scrutinise website URLs to ensure they are legitimate. Phishing websites often mimic the appearance of trusted platforms to deceive users.

- **Utilise a Designated Email Address**: Create a dedicated email address solely for cryptocurrency-related communications. By using this specific email for interactions with crypto exchanges and investment platforms, you can easily identify legitimate correspondence and detect phishing attempts targeting your financial accounts.

- **Implement Two-Factor Authentication (2FA)**: Enable 2FA on all your accounts associated with cryptocurrency investments. This additional layer of security helps prevent unauthorised access even if login credentials are compromised.

- **Educate Yourself on Phishing Tactics**: Stay informed about common phishing strategies, such as fake emails, messages, and websites designed to deceive users. Be cautious of unsolicited communications requesting sensitive information or urgent actions.

- **Regularly Update Security Software**: Keep your devices and security software up to date to mitigate vulnerabilities that scammers may exploit for phishing attacks.

- **Exercise Caution with Attachments and Links**: Avoid clicking on suspicious links or downloading attachments from unknown sources, as they may contain malware or lead to phishing websites.

These measures protect investments from phishing attacks and ensure a more secure digital environment.

Using Personal Wallets

In the world of cryptocurrency investments and trading, securing digital assets is paramount for investors. Cryptocurrencies are stored in digital wallets, which can be likened to the digital equivalent of a bank account. However, unlike traditional bank accounts, where the institution can often recover lost funds, if investors lose access to their cryptocurrency wallet or it gets hacked, their digital assets might be lost forever.

Understanding the types of wallets available and selecting the right one based on investment habits and security needs is crucial for them. Here is a deeper dive into the types of wallets and considerations for selecting one:

Software Wallets

Software wallets are applications that investors can download on their computers or mobile devices. They are designed to store private keys (a critical piece of information used to authorise outgoing transactions on the blockchain network) on the device.

Key points to consider include:

- **Accessibility**: Software wallets are highly accessible, making them convenient for traders and investors who need to make frequent transactions. Investors can easily send, receive, and manage their cryptocurrencies within the app.

- **Security Considerations**: While software wallets are more secure than keeping assets on an exchange, they are still vulnerable to online threats such as hacking, malware, and phishing attacks. It is essential for investors to ensure that their device's security is up to date and to use strong, unique passwords. Additionally, looking for wallets that offer two-factor authentication (2FA) adds an extra layer of security.

- **Reputation and Reliability**: Investors should choose a software wallet from a reputable provider known for its security and customer support. Researching and reading reviews from other users can help gauge their experiences.

Hardware Wallets

Hardware wallets are physical devices that store private keys offline. They are considered one of the safest options for storing cryptocurrencies, especially for large amounts or long-term investments. Popular examples include Ledger and Trezor.

Some aspects to consider include:

- **Enhanced Security**: Hardware wallets' primary advantage is their ability to keep private keys completely offline, making them immune to online hacking attempts. Transactions are signed within the device and then broadcast to the network, ensuring keys never leave the device.

- **Convenience vs. Security**: While hardware wallets offer superior security, they are less convenient for frequent trading compared to software wallets. Each transaction requires connecting the device to a computer or mobile device, although newer models offer Bluetooth connectivity for added convenience.

- **Cost**: Unlike software wallets, which are usually free, hardware wallets come at a cost. However, the investment is generally considered worthwhile for the enhanced security they provide, especially for those holding a significant amount of cryptocurrency.

Additional Considerations

- **Backup and Recovery**: Both software and hardware wallets typically offer a recovery phrase (a series of words) during the setup process. This phrase is crucial for recovering a wallet and funds if the device is lost, stolen, or damaged. Investors need to keep this recovery phrase in a secure, offline location.

- **Multi-Signature Support**: Some wallets offer a multi-signature feature, requiring multiple approvals before making a transaction. This adds an additional layer of security, particularly useful for businesses or investment groups.

- **User Experience**: The wallet's user interface and ease of use should be considered. A well-designed interface can make managing cryptocurrency holdings more straightforward and reduce the risk of making transaction mistakes.

In summary, selecting the right wallet is critical for any cryptocurrency investor or trader. Balancing the need for security with the convenience of making transactions is key.

Whether opting for a software wallet for its accessibility and ease of use or a hardware wallet for its unmatched security, conducting thorough research, considering specific needs, and always following best practices for securing digital assets are essential steps.

Custodial vs. Non-Custodial Wallets

There are two main types of cryptocurrency wallets: custodial and non-custodial. Custodial wallets are managed by third-party service providers, who hold the private keys to the wallet. On the other hand, non-custodial wallets give users complete control over their private keys and funds, which enhances security and privacy.

Investors should consider the trade-offs between convenience and security when choosing between custodial and non-custodial wallets. Custodial wallets may offer user-friendly interfaces and customer support, but they also pose a higher risk of hacking or losing funds. Non-custodial wallets provide greater security and control over assets, but users must manage their private keys responsibly.

Selecting the right wallet type is crucial for safeguarding cryptocurrency holdings and ensuring secure storage of digital assets.

Read-only Wallets

A distinctive category in cryptocurrency investments alongside software and hardware wallets is "read-only wallets." These wallets serve a specialised function for cryptocurrency investors and traders, enabling them to track and visualise their portfolios without necessitating the actual storage of their cryptocurrencies within the wallet itself.

Following is an expanded explanation of how read-only wallets operate and the advantages they offer:

Read-Only Wallets Explained

Read-only wallets are applications or platforms that allow investors to monitor the balances and transactions of their cryptocurrency holdings across various addresses and potentially across different blockchains. This is achieved without requiring access to the investor's private keys or the capability to initiate transactions. Investors input the public addresses of their cryptocurrency holdings, and the wallet aggregates this information, displaying an up-to-date view of their portfolio.

Key Features and Benefits

- **Security**: Read-only wallets do not require private keys or transactional permissions, eliminating the risk of fund loss due to hacking or mismanagement of keys. This characteristic renders them an excellent tool for securely monitoring investments.

- **Portfolio Tracking and Management**: Maintaining an overview of their entire portfolio can be challenging for investors who diversify their holdings across multiple cryptocurrencies and wallets. Read-only wallets provide a consolidated view of all investments, simplifying performance analysis, tracking gains or losses, and facilitating informed decision-making.

- **Simulating Transactions**: Certain read-only wallets have features that enable investors to simulate transactions. This functionality can be invaluable for strategising investment approaches or comprehending the potential impact of future trades on the portfolio, all without the risk associated with actual funds.

- **Market Insights and Alerts**: Besides portfolio tracking, many read-only wallets offer market data, news, and alerts concerning price movements or significant events. This feature assists investors in staying informed and responding promptly to market dynamics.

Choosing a Read-Only Wallet

When it comes to selecting a read-only wallet, investors should consider the following factors:

- **Supported Cryptocurrencies and Blockchains**: It is crucial to ensure that the wallet supports all the cryptocurrencies and blockchains in which the investor has stakes. Some wallets may provide broader support than others.

- **Features and Tools**: Investors should seek out wallets that offer the necessary features, such as detailed performance analytics, transaction simulations, or real-time market data.

- **Privacy and Security**: Although read-only wallets inherently secure funds, privacy concerns may still arise. Investors are advised to review the wallet's privacy policy to understand how their data is utilised and safeguarded.

- **User Experience**: The usability and intuitiveness of the app or platform can significantly enhance an investor's ability to monitor and manage their portfolio effectively. Thus, the wallet's design and user interface are important considerations.

Integrating a read-only wallet into one's cryptocurrency management strategy offers a secure and comprehensive method for monitoring investments. By providing a detailed and consolidated view of the portfolio, along with valuable market insights and the capability to simulate transactions, read-only wallets emerge as a powerful tool for both novice and seasoned investors seeking to navigate the complex landscape of cryptocurrency investing with confidence and clarity.

System Security for Investor Actions

System security is paramount for cryptocurrency investors when conducting any crypto-related activities. Ensuring that the system used is secure and clean encompasses several crucial practices:

- **Utilising a Dedicated Computer**: Cryptocurrency investors should ideally operate on a device specifically designated for trading and managing cryptocurrencies. This approach minimises the risk of security breaches by isolating the investment activities from everyday computing tasks. A dedicated device can be optimised for security, reducing the likelihood of exposure to malicious software and attacks.

- **Avoiding Public WiFi and Dubious Software Downloads**: Investors must steer clear of public WiFi networks and refrain from downloading unverified software. Public networks are notoriously insecure, offering an easy gateway for hackers to intercept data, including sensitive financial information. Similarly, downloading software from untrustworthy sources can introduce malware into the system, compromising security. Cryptocurrency investors should always use secure, private networks and only download software from reputable sources.

- **Conducting Regular Updates and Security Checks**: Keeping the system and all security software up-to-date is critical for protecting

against new and evolving threats. Cybersecurity is a dynamic field, with new vulnerabilities discovered regularly. By ensuring that the operating system and all applications, especially those related to security, are updated promptly, investors can safeguard against known vulnerabilities. Regular security checks and scans for malware are also essential in identifying and mitigating potential threats before they can cause harm.

Adhering to these system security practices is essential for safeguarding cryptocurrency investments. Cryptocurrencies' digital nature makes them particularly susceptible to online threats. By taking proactive measures to secure their systems, investors can significantly reduce the risk of security breaches, ensuring their investments remain protected.

Conclusion

In conclusion, maintaining control and security in cryptocurrency investments is paramount for investors looking to safeguard their assets and navigate the complexities of the digital asset space. By choosing reputable exchanges, implementing robust security practices, and utilising secure wallet management strategies, investors can mitigate risks associated with hacks, data breaches, and regulatory compliance.

Understanding the importance of security measures, compliance with regulations, and transparency in financial transactions is essential for ensuring the long-term success and protection of cryptocurrency investments.

By staying informed, proactive, and diligent in their security practices, investors can enhance the security and integrity of their digital assets while engaging in the dynamic world of cryptocurrencies.

Questions & Answers

Q **What are the key considerations for retaining control and security in cryptocurrency investments?**

   A Retaining control of private keys, implementing strong security practices, and monitoring account activity are essential for maintaining security in cryptocurrency investments.

Q **How can investors ensure the security of their digital assets when using personal wallets?**

   A Investors can enhance the security of their digital assets by using software wallets with strong security features and hardware wallets for offline storage of private keys.

Q **What factors should investors research when choosing and using cryptocurrency exchanges safely?**

   A Investors should research reputable exchanges, understand deposit and withdrawal processes, and prioritise security features like cold storage and encryption protocols for safe cryptocurrency transactions.

Q **What are the benefits of utilising read-only wallets to monitor cryptocurrency investments?**

   A Read-only wallets provide a secure way to track balances and transactions across multiple addresses and blockchains without the ability to initiate transactions, enhancing security and portfolio management.

Q **What security practices should investors follow to protect their investments when conducting crypto-related activities?**

   A Using dedicated devices, avoiding public WiFi, and updating systems and security software are crucial security practices for protecting cryptocurrency investments.

Q How can investors enhance system security to safeguard their cryptocurrency investments effectively?

A Investors can enhance system security and protect their investments by using dedicated computers for crypto activities, avoiding public WiFi, and conducting regular security checks and updates.

Q Why must investors understand the functionality and advantages of read-only wallets in managing their portfolios securely?

A Understanding read-only wallets helps investors securely monitor their investments without compromising security, providing insights into portfolio performance and market dynamics.

Chapter 17

Regulatory Updates & Compliance in Crypto Investments

Understanding Regulatory Landscape

The regulatory landscape for cryptocurrencies is complex and varies significantly across different jurisdictions. Investors in the cryptocurrency sector must navigate a maze of laws and regulations that can impact their trading activities.

These regulations often pertain to securities law, anti-money laundering (AML) requirements, and other financial services regulations.

Compliance obligations include registering with relevant financial authorities, adhering to reporting requirements, and maintaining appropriate records. Staying informed about regulatory changes is crucial for investors to ensure that their investment activities remain legal and compliant with the latest standards set by regulatory bodies.

Taxation Considerations

It is important to consider the tax implications of cryptocurrency transactions as part of an investment strategy. In many countries, cryptocurrencies are treated as property for tax purposes, meaning that capital gains tax applies to any profits from selling or exchanging the asset. Moreover, income tax may apply to earnings from cryptocurrency mining or other forms of receipt.

Investors must keep detailed records of their transactions, including dates, amounts, market values, and the purpose of each transaction, to accurately report their liabilities and comply with local tax regulations.

AML/KYC Compliance

Following Anti-Money Laundering (AML) and Know-Your-Customer (KYC) regulations is imperative to maintaining the integrity of financial systems and avoiding the misuse of cryptocurrencies for illegal activities. When registering with exchanges or trading platforms, investors may be required to undergo identity verification procedures, and these entities must conduct due diligence to monitor and report suspicious activities.

These compliance measures protect investors by ensuring that their preferred platforms uphold legal standards and contribute to the prevention of fraud, money laundering, and terrorism financing.

Security Regulations and Best Practices

Compliance with cybersecurity and data protection regulations is paramount to safeguarding investments in the digital asset space. Investors should ensure their chosen platforms comply with industry data security standards, such as encryption, secure socket layers, and robust authentication mechanisms.

Adhering to best practices such as regular software updates, using two-factor authentication, and employing cold storage for large balances can further enhance security. Regulatory bodies in many jurisdictions are increasingly focusing on cryptocurrency platforms' security practices, making compliance a moving target that requires constant vigilance.

Cryptocurrency Regulations by Region

Investing in cryptocurrencies can be complicated due to the regulatory differences between jurisdictions. Regulations vary widely between countries, affecting cryptocurrency trading, taxation, and monitoring.

To avoid legal pitfalls and ensure compliance, investors must be aware of the regulatory landscape in each jurisdiction where they operate. This may require consulting with legal experts in cryptocurrency regulations or using specialised compliance services that can provide guidance and support in adhering to international laws.

Global Regulatory Variances

Regional regulations play a significant role in shaping investment strategies in the cryptocurrency market. Understanding the diverse landscape of cryptocurrency regulations across regions and jurisdictions is crucial for investors. It ensures compliance and helps manage risk. Factors such as licensing requirements, tax implications, and legal frameworks can vary widely, influencing investment strategies and operational practices. This underscores the need for investors to be cautious and attentive to the regulatory environment.

Staying informed about regulatory developments in key regions such as the United States, European Union, Asia-Pacific, and other significant markets is not just important, it's a responsibility of cryptocurrency investors. Each region may have its own rules governing cryptocurrency exchanges, initial coin offerings (ICOs), and anti-money laundering (AML) practices. By being aware of these regulations, investors can proactively navigate the legal environment and make informed decisions that align with compliance standards, thereby contributing to a healthy and sustainable cryptocurrency market.

Conclusion

Understanding the regulatory landscape is crucial for successful cryptocurrency investing. Regulations vary significantly across jurisdictions, so investors must proactively comprehend and comply with securities-related laws, anti-money laundering (AML), know-your-customer (KYC) procedures, and taxation. Adhering to these regulations ensures the legality of investment activities and contributes to the integrity and stability of the financial system.

Taxation, AML/KYC obligations, and cybersecurity best practices are essential aspects of regulatory compliance. They require diligent record-keeping and ongoing awareness of regulatory updates. Investors should stay informed about regional regulatory differences and seek expert advice when necessary to ensure compliance with international laws.

Overall, by staying informed and compliant with evolving regulations, cryptocurrency investors can safeguard their investments, improve security, and contribute to a sustainable and transparent market environment. This chapter emphasises the importance of thoroughly understanding regulatory requirements, which ultimately assists investors in making informed, compliant, and strategic decisions in their cryptocurrency investment journey.

Questions & Answers

Q Why is it important for cryptocurrency investors to stay informed about regulatory updates?

> **A** Staying informed about regulatory updates is crucial for cryptocurrency investors to ensure compliance with evolving laws and regulations, mitigate legal risks, and adapt their investment strategies to changing regulatory environments.

Q How can global regulatory variances impact cryptocurrency investments?

> **A** Global regulatory variances can significantly impact cryptocurrency investments by influencing trading activities, taxation requirements, and compliance standards. Understanding these differences is essential for investors to navigate legal complexities and ensure regulatory compliance.

Q What are the key compliance concerns related to cryptocurrency transactions for investors?

> **A** Key compliance concerns for investors in cryptocurrency transactions include anti-money laundering (AML) regulations, know-your-customer (KYC) requirements, and security protocols. Adhering to these compliance measures is essential to prevent illicit activities and maintain transparency in financial transactions.

Q How can investors mitigate risks associated with compliance issues in cryptocurrency investments?

> **A** Investors can mitigate risks related to compliance issues by conducting thorough due diligence, maintaining clear records of transactions, and seeking guidance from legal experts specialising in cryptocurrency regulations. Proactive compliance measures can help investors navigate regulatory challenges effectively.

Chapter 18

Regulatory Updates and Investment Insights for Stablecoins

Stablecoins have become an essential part of the world of cryptocurrencies, as they offer the advantages of digital currency usage along with stability, which is not commonly found in other cryptocurrencies like Bitcoin and Ethereum. They are designed to be tied to stable assets like fiat currencies such as the US dollar, making them a favourable alternative for trading and remittances and a secure way to store value.

However, as stablecoins are becoming more popular, regulatory authorities from different countries are paying more attention to them, making it crucial to stay informed about the developing regulatory environment.

Understanding the Regulatory Framework

Global regulators focus on defining and categorising stablecoins to ensure they comply with traditional financial frameworks. Classifying stablecoins as either e-money, securities, or commodities impacts their regulation and the necessary compliance measures for their operation.

The clarity of this classification is essential for investors to navigate the market effectively and remain compliant.

Reserve Management and Transparency

One of the main regulatory concerns in the cryptocurrency industry is the management of reserves that support stablecoins. To ensure stability, issuers must maintain full reserves in highly liquid assets. Recent cases such as the Tether settlement have resulted in increased scrutiny, highlighting the importance of transparency in reserve compositions and regular audits.

By understanding these requirements, investors can better assess the stability and reliability of various stablecoin offerings.

Compliance with AML and KYC Regulations

Stablecoin transactions are now being closely monitored due to the implementation of Anti-Money Laundering (AML) and Know-Your-Customer (KYC) regulations. To comply with these regulations, stablecoin issuers and related exchanges must have strong AML and KYC protocols. Investors must know these regulatory requirements for legal involvement and risk management in the stablecoin market.

The Role of International Cooperation and CBDCs

The decentralised nature of cryptocurrencies demands cooperation among international regulators. Organisations such as the Financial Action Task Force (FATF) and G7 are taking initiatives to standardise regulations, which will ensure a consistent approach to the governance of stablecoins. Moreover, the emergence of Central Bank Digital Currencies (CBDCs) is affecting the regulatory framework. This could result in stricter regulations to maintain the stability of financial systems and prevent disruption to monetary policies.

Future Trends and Investment Opportunities

In the near future, the rules and regulations governing stablecoins are likely to undergo further changes. While this may pose some challenges, it also presents new opportunities. Clear regulations can open up new investment prospects, allowing investors to identify new trends and potential partnerships. Additionally, having a good understanding of these developments can help with risk management and strategic investment planning.

Importance of Regulatory Insights for Investors

Understanding the details of stablecoin regulations is crucial for cryptocurrency investors. It guarantees compliance with current laws and helps in making strategic decisions. Keeping track of regulatory updates can improve investment strategies, diversify investment portfolios, and reduce potential risks associated with regulation changes.

Conclusion

The inclusion of regulatory knowledge on stablecoins in investment strategies is highly beneficial. It provides investors the resources to navigate the intricate and ever-changing regulatory systems, take advantage of emerging prospects, and maintain conformity in a dynamic market.

Staying informed and adaptable will be crucial to successful and compliant cryptocurrency investing as the situation evolves.

Questions & Answers

Q What are the key components of AML and KYC regulations that investors need to understand in the cryptocurrency market?

   A Investors need to grasp the importance of conducting thorough research, complying with anti-money laundering (AML) and know-your-customer (KYC) regulations, and implementing security measures to prevent illicit activities and ensure regulatory compliance.

Q Why must investors conduct thorough research and comply with anti-money laundering (AML) and know-your-customer (KYC) regulations in cryptocurrency investments?

   A Conducting thorough research and complying with AML and KYC regulations are essential to preventing illicit activities, ensuring transaction transparency, and adhering to regulatory standards.

Q What are the key considerations discussed in the section about security regulations and best practices in Chapter 15?

   A The section covers aspects such as data security standards, best practices like regular software updates and two-factor authentication, and the importance of following industry security standards to protect investments.

Q How can compliance with cybersecurity and data protection regulations enhance the security of cryptocurrency investments?

   A Compliance with cybersecurity and data protection regulations can enhance security by implementing encryption, secure authentication mechanisms, and following best practices to prevent unauthorised access and protect sensitive information.

Q   Why must investors understand the global regulatory variances in different jurisdictions when engaging in cryptocurrency investments?

   A   Understanding global regulatory variances helps investors comply with local laws, regulations, and taxation requirements, ensuring legal operation and minimising risks associated with non-compliance.

Q   What potential risks are associated with non-compliance with AML and KYC regulations in cryptocurrency investments?

   A   Non-compliance with AML and KYC regulations can expose investors to legal risks, financial penalties, and reputational damage and increase their likelihood of involvement in illicit activities.

Q   How can staying informed about regulatory updates and changes in AML and KYC regulations benefit investors in the cryptocurrency market?

   A   Staying informed about regulatory updates helps investors maintain compliance, mitigate risks, and adapt to AML and KYC regulations changes, ensuring legal and secure participation in the market.

Chapter 19

Crypto-Friendly Banking and Payment Strategies

Cryptocurrencies offer a decentralised and innovative approach to financial transactions. However, it's important to recognise that traditional banking institutions may not always support cryptocurrency activities. Depending on the jurisdiction and country, individuals engaging in cryptocurrency transactions may encounter obstacles when using their bank accounts to fund crypto exchanges or withdraw cash from crypto-related activities.

Certain banks in specific regions have been known to impose restrictions or create issues for customers involved in cryptocurrency transactions. These challenges can range from account closures to transaction processing delays or even freezing of funds. Investors should be aware of the potential risks and limitations imposed by traditional financial institutions when dealing with the intersection of traditional banking and cryptocurrency activities.

Establishing Relationships with Crypto-Friendly Banks:

In today's ever-changing financial landscape, it is crucial to identify banks that are open to cryptocurrency transactions. Here are some strategies for establishing connections with banks that are crypto-friendly:

1. **Research and Due Diligence**: Comprehensive research is key to pinpointing banks that view cryptocurrency transactions favourably. Seek out financial institutions that openly endorse crypto businesses or have policies that cater to crypto investors.

2.   **Engage with Digital Banks and Challenger Banks**: Digital and challenger banks are often more receptive to innovative financial technologies like cryptocurrencies. Consider establishing accounts with these entities to access crypto-friendly services and avoid potential clashes with traditional banks.

3.   **Dedicated Crypto Accounts**: Establishing a separate bank account specifically for cryptocurrency transactions can help segregate crypto-related activities from traditional banking operations. Investors can minimise the impact on their primary bank accounts by using this dedicated account to fund payment processors and withdraw fiat from crypto investments.

4.   **Seek Recommendations from the Crypto Community**: Networking within the cryptocurrency community can provide valuable insights into banks that are open to crypto-related activities. Online forums, social media groups, and industry events are excellent platforms to seek recommendations and experiences from other crypto investors.

Considerations When Dealing with Crypto-Friendly Banks

Establishing relationships with crypto-friendly banks can provide convenience and support for cryptocurrency transactions. However, it's essential that cryptocurrency investors be aware of certain considerations to effectively navigate potential challenges:

1.   **Transparency and Compliance**: Ensure transparency in cryptocurrency activities and comply with all regulatory requirements. Crypto-friendly banks may have specific compliance standards, such as providing detailed transaction information or verifying the source of funds.

     Investors must communicate openly with their traditional banks about their cryptocurrency activities. Providing clear explanations of the source of funds and the nature of transactions can help mitigate concerns and demonstrate the legitimacy of the funds being transferred to and from payment processors.

2. **Account Monitoring and Reporting**: Crypto-friendly banks are likely to scrutinise and monitor cryptocurrency investors' accounts closely. Cryptocurrency investors should monitor their transactions regularly, report any suspicious activities promptly, and maintain clear records to comply with anti-money laundering regulations.

Finding Intermediary Payment Processors

In situations where direct transactions between cryptocurrency exchanges and traditional banks face obstacles, intermediary payment processors can serve as valuable solutions. Here's how investors can find and engage with these processors:

1. **Research Payment Processing Services**: Explore reliable payment processing services that specialise in facilitating transactions between crypto platforms and traditional banks. Look for providers with a track record of reliability and compliance with financial regulations.

2. **Review Terms and Conditions**: Before working with an intermediary payment processor, cryptocurrency investors should carefully review its terms and conditions. They should note fees, transaction limits, processing times, and any restrictions on cryptocurrency transactions to ensure they meet their needs.

Examples of Payment Processors

Here are some examples of payment processors that cater to cryptocurrency transactions and may fit the description of intermediary payment processors for engaging with crypto-friendly banks:

- **BitPay**: BitPay is a well-known payment processor that allows businesses to accept cryptocurrency payments and settle in fiat currency. It provides services for Bitcoin and other major cryptocurrencies, facilitating seamless transactions for merchants.

- **Coinbase Commerce**: Coinbase Commerce is a payment solution offered by the popular cryptocurrency exchange Coinbase. It enables businesses to accept various cryptocurrencies as payment for goods and services, with the option to convert funds into fiat currency.

- **CoinPayments**: CoinPayments is a global cryptocurrency payment gateway that supports over 2.340 cryptocurrencies. It offers merchants a range of services, including payment processing, shopping cart plugins, and integration with popular e-commerce platforms.

- **GoCoin**: GoCoin is a payment processor specialising in cryptocurrency transactions for merchants. It supports Bitcoin, Ethereum, Litecoin, and other digital assets and provides secure payment processing solutions for online businesses.

- **Skrill**: Skrill, formerly known as Moneybookers, is a digital wallet and payment platform that allows users to buy, sell, and hold cryptocurrencies. It offers services for converting cryptocurrencies into fiat currency and vice versa, along with options for online payments and transfers.

Here's a detailed explanation of how these payment processors may enable seamless transactions for both investors and businesses:

1. **Investing in Cryptocurrencies**: Individuals and corporations can use these payment processors to purchase cryptocurrencies by selecting the desired digital assets and completing the transaction through the platform. Users can fund their accounts with FIAT currency, which is then converted into cryptocurrencies at the current exchange rate.

2. **Accepting Cryptocurrency Payments**: For businesses, these payment processors allow the acceptance of cryptocurrency payments for goods and services. Upon receiving a crypto payment, the

processor converts the digital assets into FIAT currency, which is then deposited into the merchant's bank account.

3. **Converting Crypto to FIAT**: When individuals or businesses wish to convert their cryptocurrency holdings back to FIAT currency, they can initiate the process through the payment processor. The platform facilitates the sale of cryptocurrencies at the prevailing market rate and transfers the equivalent FIAT amount to the user's linked bank account.

4. **Transaction Settlement**: Payment processors typically handle the conversion and settlement process internally, ensuring that users receive the appropriate FIAT amount corresponding to their cryptocurrency holdings. The conversion rates are transparent, and users can track the status of their transactions through the platform.

5. **Security and Compliance**: Payment processors prioritise security measures to safeguard users' funds and personal information. They adhere to regulatory requirements, including anti-money laundering (AML) and know-your-customer (KYC) procedures, to ensure compliance with financial regulations and prevent illicit activities.

6. **User-Friendly Interface**: These payment processors offer user-friendly interfaces that simplify the process of investing in cryptocurrencies and converting funds back to FIAT. Users can easily navigate the platform, view transaction histories, and manage their crypto holdings with ease.

By leveraging these payment processors, individuals and corporations can seamlessly engage in cryptocurrency investments, accept crypto payments, and convert their digital assets to FIAT currency when needed.

The platforms provide a convenient and secure way to navigate the complexities of the crypto market while ensuring compliance with regulatory standards and facilitating efficient financial transactions.

Considerations When Using Intermediary Payment Processors

When using intermediary payment processors for cryptocurrency transactions, it's important to consider the following factors in order to effectively navigate potential challenges:

1. **Security and Data Protection**: Cryptocurrency investors should remember to prioritise payment processors that implement robust security measures to protect their financial information and transactions. They should verify that the processor complies with data protection regulations to reduce the risk of unauthorised access or data breaches.

2. **Transaction Transparency**: Cryptocurrency investors should choose payment processors that provide transparent transaction processes and clear documentation. Understanding how their transactions are processed and recorded can help them track their financial activities and address any discrepancies effectively.

3. **Banking Relationships**: If investors fund their accounts on these payment processors using traditional banks that have anti-cryptocurrency policies or are not crypto-friendly, there may be a risk of account closures or restrictions. Some banks have been known to flag transactions related to cryptocurrencies, leading to account freezes or closures.

4. **FIAT Withdrawals**: When investors cash out their cryptocurrency holdings to FIAT currency and transfer the funds to their traditional bank accounts, there could be potential issues if the bank views the source of funds as suspicious or related to cryptocurrency activities. This could result in delays in processing withdrawals or even account scrutiny.

5. **Compliance Concerns**: Traditional banks may have compliance concerns related to cryptocurrency transactions, especially if they suspect money laundering or other illicit activities. If a bank detects a high volume of transactions from cryptocurrency-related sources, it may raise red flags and subject the investor's account to additional scrutiny.

6. **Mitigating Risks**: To mitigate these risks, investors should consider using crypto-friendly banks or financial institutions for their cryptocurrency-related transactions. They can also maintain clear records of their transactions and provide explanations to their traditional banks if needed to demonstrate the legitimacy of their funds.

7. **Alternative Funding Sources**: Investors can explore alternative funding sources for their cryptocurrency activities, such as using dedicated accounts or payment methods specifically for crypto transactions. This separation can help prevent potential issues with traditional banks that may not be supportive of cryptocurrency-related activities.

Conclusion

In summary, while using payment processors for cryptocurrency transactions funded from traditional banks can pose risks, investors can take proactive steps to mitigate these risks by being transparent, using crypto-friendly financial institutions, and maintaining clear records of their transactions.

By understanding and addressing these potential challenges, individuals and businesses can navigate the complexities of the crypto market more effectively, establish relationships with crypto-friendly banks, leverage intermediary payment processors, and ensure compliance with regulatory requirements while engaging in cryptocurrency transactions.

Questions & Answers

Q **Why is it important for investors to establish relationships with crypto-friendly banks?**

A Establishing relationships with crypto-friendly banks is crucial for investors to avoid potential obstacles when engaging in cryptocurrency transactions. These banks are more receptive to crypto-related activities, reducing the risk of account closures or transaction delays.

Q **How can investors identify crypto-friendly banks?**

A Investors can identify crypto-friendly banks through comprehensive research. They should seek out financial institutions that openly support crypto businesses or cater to crypto investors. Engaging with digital and challenger banks known for their openness to innovative financial technologies is also recommended.

Q **What considerations should investors keep in mind when dealing with crypto-friendly banks?**

A Investors should prioritise transparency and compliance with regulatory requirements when dealing with crypto-friendly banks. They should communicate openly about their cryptocurrency activities, monitor their accounts closely, and report any suspicious activities promptly to ensure compliance with anti-money laundering regulations.

Q **How can intermediary payment processors help investors navigate challenges with traditional banks in cryptocurrency transactions?**

A Intermediary payment processors provide a bridge between cryptocurrency exchanges and traditional banks, offering solutions for seamless transactions. They facilitate the conversion of cryptocurrencies to fiat currency and vice versa, enabling investors to navigate potential obstacles with traditional banking institutions.

Q **What are some examples of intermediary payment processors that cater to cryptocurrency transactions?**

    A Examples of intermediary payment processors include BitPay, Coinbase Commerce, CoinPayments, GoCoin, and Skrill. These platforms specialise in facilitating cryptocurrency transactions for investors and businesses, offering services for buying, selling, and converting digital assets.

Q **How do intermediary payment processors ensure security and compliance in cryptocurrency transactions?**

    A Intermediary payment processors prioritise security measures to safeguard users' funds and personal information. They comply with regulatory requirements, including anti-money laundering (AML) and know-your-customer (KYC) procedures, to ensure compliance with financial regulations and prevent illicit activities.

Chapter 20

Tax Planning Strategies for Cryptocurrency Investors

Investing in cryptocurrency comes with its own tax challenges due to this sector's constantly changing nature of tax regulations. To deal with these challenges effectively and ensure compliance while optimising tax outcomes, investors might consider several approaches to tax planning. Here are some strategies that can help:

Keeping Detailed Records of Transactions

Keeping accurate records of all cryptocurrency transactions is essential to ensure a successful investment strategy. This includes recording the dates of transactions, the values at the time of transactions, the amounts bought or sold, and the purpose of each transaction, whether for trading, investment, or personal use. Maintaining these detailed records is crucial for accurately determining tax liabilities and can be invaluable in the event of an audit.

Understanding the Tax Implications of Crypto-to-Crypto Transactions

Investors need to be aware that exchanging one cryptocurrency for another can often result in a taxable event in many jurisdictions. Every trade or exchange carries the potential of triggering capital gains or losses, which must be reported accurately for tax purposes. Therefore, understanding this aspect of crypto trading is crucial for proper tax reporting and planning.

Utilising Tax-Loss Harvesting

Tax-loss harvesting is a tax-saving strategy that involves selling cryptocurrencies that have decreased in value to offset gains made elsewhere in an investor's portfolio. This can reduce the overall capital gains tax liability. However, investors need to be cautious of wash-sale rules. A tax claim can be disallowed if a similar asset is repurchased shortly before or after the sale. It is worth noting that wash-sale rules currently apply to stocks and securities and do not explicitly apply to cryptocurrencies in some jurisdictions. Nonetheless, as regulations evolve, this may change.

Long-Term Holding for Favourable Tax Rates

In certain regions, the tax rates on long-term capital gains are lower than those on short-term gains. Investors who hold on to their cryptocurrency for over a year before selling may take advantage of the reduced tax rates. This strategy may require patience and a long-term investment outlook, but it has the potential to decrease the tax burden significantly.

Retirement Accounts for Tax-Free or Tax-Deferred Growth

Investing in cryptocurrencies using certain retirement accounts, such as a Self-Directed IRA in the United States, can provide significant tax benefits. These include tax-free growth or tax-deferred benefits, meaning taxes can be deferred until retirement. In the case of Roth IRAs, the growth can also be tax-free.

This strategy can be particularly advantageous given the high growth potential of cryptocurrencies. However, planning carefully and adhering to the rules specific to retirement accounts is essential.

Consulting with Tax Professionals

Due to cryptocurrency taxation's intricacy and ever-evolving nature, seeking guidance from tax experts specialising in this field can be highly advantageous. These professionals can offer personalised recommendations and tactics that are based on the most up-to-date regulations and an individual's unique situation.

Conclusion

Cryptocurrency investors must plan their taxes effectively to comply with tax laws and maximise their investment returns after taxes. To achieve this, investors can use strategies such as maintaining detailed records, understanding the implications of crypto-to-crypto transactions, and utilising tax-loss harvesting. By adopting these approaches, investors can navigate the complexities of cryptocurrency taxation more efficiently.

Questions & Answers

Q **How does keeping detailed records of transactions benefit cryptocurrency investors for tax planning?**

> **A** Keeping detailed records helps investors accurately report transactions, calculate capital gains or losses, and comply with tax regulations, leading to more efficient tax planning and reporting.

Q **What are the tax implications of crypto-to-crypto transactions, and why is it essential for investors to understand them?**

> **A** Crypto-to-crypto transactions can trigger taxable events, requiring investors to report capital gains or losses. Understanding these implications is crucial for accurate tax reporting and planning.

Q **How can cryptocurrency investors utilise tax-loss harvesting to optimise tax outcomes?**

> **A** Tax-loss harvesting involves selling investments at a loss to offset gains and reduce tax liabilities. Cryptocurrency investors can strategically use this technique to manage their tax obligations effectively.

Chapter 21

Community Engagement and Networking in the Crypto Space

Importance of Community Engagement

Engagement with the cryptocurrency community offers numerous benefits, including access to a wealth of informal insights and emerging trends that are not readily available through traditional media.

For investors in the cryptocurrency market, participating in community discussions can provide early signals of market movements and innovations.

The community serves as a crucial resource for understanding the nuanced perspectives of diverse stakeholders, including developers, investors, and enthusiasts, which can inform investment strategies and risk management.

Participation in Forums and Conferences

Active participation in forums, conferences, and social media platforms is a strategic approach for staying abreast of the latest developments and market sentiments in the cryptocurrency sector. Forums like BitcoinTalk and CryptoCompare and professional networks like LinkedIn offer platforms where investors can engage in discussions, ask questions, and gain insights from experienced traders and industry experts.

Conferences provide a structured environment for deeper learning and networking. Investors can connect with innovators and thought leaders to discuss future trends, regulatory changes, and technological advancements.

Building a Network of Investors

It is essential for investors to connect with others in order to share knowledge, experiences, and insights about the market. These networks can be valuable resources for collaboration and support, particularly when dealing with cryptocurrency's volatile and complex world.

By sharing diverse experiences, investors can learn from each other's successes and mistakes, which can help them make informed decisions. Networking can occur online and offline through community meetups, online forums, or mutual connections, creating a sense of camaraderie and mutual growth.

Collaborative Learning and Knowledge Sharing

Collaborative learning and knowledge sharing through community engagement are crucial to staying up-to-date with the ever-changing cryptocurrency sector. This environment encourages sharing resources, trading strategies, and technical insights, which can significantly enhance an individual's understanding of market dynamics.

Regular interaction with the community helps investors stay informed of industry trends, regulatory updates, and technological innovations, ensuring they remain competitive and well-informed.

Case Studies in Community Engagement

Demonstrating successful community engagement can highlight the advantages of being deeply involved in the cryptocurrency community, leading to valuable investment opportunities. For example, early participants in cryptocurrency forums may have gained valuable insights into initial coin offerings (ICOs) or emerging blockchain technologies before they gained mainstream popularity.

Another case could involve a group of investors who met at a blockchain conference and formed a consortium to invest in a promising start-up. These examples show the practical benefits of community engagement in accessing information, resources, and unique opportunities that may not be available through other channels.

Conclusion

Community engagement and networking are crucial aspects of the cryptocurrency space. They provide investors with a competitive advantage through shared insights, knowledge, and opportunities. These engagements enhance an individual's investment journey and contribute to the broader knowledge and stability of the cryptocurrency market.

Questions & Answers

Q Why is community engagement important for cryptocurrency investors?

   A Community engagement provides valuable insights, early signals of market trends, and opportunities for collaboration and learning, enhancing investors' understanding and success in the cryptocurrency space.

Q How can participation in forums and conferences benefit cryptocurrency investors?

   A Participation in forums and conferences allows investors to stay informed about industry developments, network with peers, and gain knowledge from experts, contributing to informed decision-making and strategic planning.

Q What are the advantages of building a network of investors in the cryptocurrency space?

   A Building a network of investors enables knowledge sharing, collaboration, and access to diverse perspectives and opportunities, fostering growth, learning, and potential partnerships in the cryptocurrency market.

Chapter 22

Psychology of Investing in Cryptocurrencies

Understanding Investor Psychology

Investor psychology significantly impacts decision-making in the volatile cryptocurrency market. Psychological biases such as overconfidence, confirmation bias, and loss aversion can play a crucial role in influencing investment choices.

Overconfidence can make investors underestimate risks and invest too much in speculative ventures. Confirmation bias can lead them to seek information that confirms their beliefs while ignoring contradictory evidence. Loss aversion can discourage investors from selling underperforming assets to avoid realising losses, which can result in even more significant losses.

Recognising these emotional influences is the first step towards mitigating their impact on investment decisions.

Managing Emotional Biases

Investors in cryptocurrencies need to be aware of their emotional biases, as they can significantly impact investment decisions. For example, the fear of missing out (FOMO) can cause investors to make impulsive decisions without adequate research, leading to poor investment outcomes. Similarly, sudden market downturns can trigger panic selling, resulting in substantial losses.

To manage these biases, investors can establish predetermined investment goals and criteria for entering and exiting positions. This structured approach helps maintain objectivity and reduces the likelihood of decisions driven solely by emotions.

Discipline and Patience in Investing

Maintaining discipline and patience is essential for achieving long-term success in cryptocurrency investing. The market is known for its sharp fluctuations, which can test the resolve of even the most experienced investors.

By adhering to a well-thought-out investment strategy and resisting the urge to react impulsively to short-term market movements, investors can improve their chances of realising substantial returns over time.

Patience allows investors to ride out market volatility and benefit from significant trends rather than attempting to capitalise on short-term fluctuations.

Navigating Emotional Market Dynamics in Cryptocurrency Investing

Investing in cryptocurrencies involves navigating not only the technical aspects of the market but also the psychological challenges that come with volatile price movements and market uncertainties. Understanding and managing emotional biases are crucial for making informed investment decisions. This section explores critical emotional market dynamics that can impact cryptocurrency investors and strategies to navigate them effectively.

- **Fear, Uncertainty, Doubt (FUD)**: Fear, Uncertainty, and Doubt (FUD) is a common phenomenon in the cryptocurrency market. Negative information or rumours create fear and uncertainty among investors, which can lead to panic selling and market downturns. It is crucial for investors to recognise FUD and develop strategies to mitigate its impact on their investment decisions.

By staying informed and conducting thorough research, investors can navigate through FUD-induced market fluctuations with confidence.

Example: In 2017, during the China crypto ban, fear, uncertainty, and doubt (FUD) quickly spread, leading to a sharp decline in cryptocurrency prices. Investors who sold their holdings in panic suffered losses, while those who remained well-informed and understood the regulatory environment successfully navigated the turbulent market caused by FUD.

- **Fear of Missing Out (FOMO)**: Fear of Missing Out (FOMO) is a psychological bias that drives investors to make impulsive decisions based on the fear of missing out on potential gains in a rapidly rising market. Managing FOMO involves setting predetermined investment goals and criteria for entering and exiting positions.

  By establishing a structured approach to decision-making, investors can avoid falling prey to FOMO-induced trading behaviours and make informed investment choices aligned with their financial objectives.

  Example: The FOMO surrounding the ICO craze in 2017 resulted in many investors participating in projects without proper due diligence. This led to numerous scams and failed projects, underscoring the importance of managing FOMO and making informed investment decisions.

- **All-Time High (ATH)**: All-Time High (ATH) represents the highest price level a cryptocurrency has ever reached. Investors often face psychological challenges when prices hit ATH, such as indecision on whether to buy, sell, or hold. It is essential for investors to maintain discipline and patience during ATH scenarios, focusing on long-term investment goals rather than short-term price movements.

  By understanding the psychological impact of ATH and adhering to a well-thought-out investment strategy, investors can navigate ATH situations with resilience.

Example: When Bitcoin reached its all-time high (ATH) in 2021, some investors hesitated to sell because they feared missing out on potential gains. Understanding the psychological impact of reaching an all-time high and having a clear exit strategy could have helped investors capitalise on their profits or protect themselves against market corrections.

- **Greed**: Greed can drive investors to take excessive risks or chase unrealistic returns in the cryptocurrency market. Recognizing and managing greed is crucial for making rational investment decisions.

  By setting realistic investment goals, conducting thorough research, and avoiding impulsive behaviours driven by greed, investors can maintain a disciplined approach to investing and mitigate the risks associated with greed-induced trading strategies.

  Example: The Bitconnect Ponzi scheme is a classic example of how greed can lead investors to fall for unrealistic promises of high returns. Many investors suffered significant financial losses due to greed-driven decisions, highlighting the importance of remaining cautious and avoiding schemes that appear too good to be true.

- **Panic Selling**: Panic selling occurs when investors react impulsively to market downturns, leading to mass sell-offs and price declines. Managing panic selling involves:
  - Staying informed about market trends.
  - Maintaining a diversified portfolio.
  - Adhering to a well-defined investment strategy.

  By avoiding knee-jerk reactions and focusing on long-term objectives, investors can navigate market volatility and avoid the pitfalls of panic-induced selling behaviours.

  Example: During the COVID-19 market crash in March 2020, panic selling led to a sharp decline in cryptocurrency prices. Investors who gave in to panic selling missed out on the subsequent market recovery, which emphasises the negative impact of emotional decision-making during turbulent market conditions.

- **Market Manipulation**: Market manipulation involves intentionally deceiving or influencing market prices for personal gain. Recognizing signs of market manipulation and safeguarding against fraudulent activities is essential for protecting investments.

  By conducting due diligence, staying vigilant against suspicious market behaviours, and seeking reputable sources of information, investors can mitigate the risks associated with market manipulation and make informed investment decisions based on reliable data and analysis.

  Example: The collapse of the Mt. Gox exchange in 2014 due to fraudulent activities and market manipulation is a cautionary tale for investors. Understanding the signs of market manipulation and conducting thorough research can help investors protect their assets and avoid falling victim to fraudulent schemes.

Stress Management Techniques

Investing in cryptocurrencies can be a stressful experience due to the market's high volatility and unpredictability. Therefore, investors must develop effective stress management techniques to ensure clear-headed decision-making. Mindfulness meditation, regular physical exercise, and maintaining a balanced lifestyle are some of the techniques that can help manage stress.

Additionally, setting clear boundaries for trading hours and ensuring sufficient downtime can prevent burnout and keep the psychological pressures of trading in check. By implementing these strategies, investors can minimise the negative impacts of stress and improve their overall well-being.

Case Studies in Investor Psychology

Real-life examples of how investor psychology affects cryptocurrency trading outcomes can offer valuable lessons. For instance, during the cryptocurrency boom in 2017, many investors exhibited extreme greed. This led to a bubble that eventually burst, causing significant losses for those who invested at peak prices.

Another scenario could involve an investor who experienced initial losses but stuck to a disciplined investment strategy. As a result, they experienced significant gains as the market recovered. These case studies emphasise the importance of understanding and managing psychological factors while making investment decisions.

Conclusion

Exploring the various aspects of investor psychology can help cryptocurrency traders develop a more disciplined and rational approach to trading, ultimately enhancing their ability to achieve long-term success in this dynamic market. To achieve this, it is crucial to understand and manage emotional biases, maintain discipline, practice patience, and employ effective stress management strategies. All these components are essential elements of a robust psychological framework for investing in cryptocurrencies.

Questions & Answers

Q **Why is understanding investor psychology important in cryptocurrency investments?**

    A Understanding investor psychology helps investors recognise and manage emotional biases, make rational decisions, and effectively navigate the volatile cryptocurrency market.

Q **How can managing emotional biases benefit cryptocurrency investors?**

    A Managing emotional biases like fear of missing out (FOMO) and panic selling can prevent impulsive decisions, leading to more strategic and disciplined investment choices with better long-term outcomes.

Q **Why are discipline and patience essential in cryptocurrency investing?**

    A Discipline and patience help investors stick to their trading plans, avoid emotional decision-making, and withstand market volatility, leading to more consistent and successful investment strategies.

Q **How can fear of missing out (FOMO) influence investment decisions in the cryptocurrency market?**

    A Fear of missing out (FOMO) can lead investors to make impulsive decisions based on the fear of missing out on potential gains, often resulting in buying assets at inflated prices.

Q **What role does discipline play in successful cryptocurrency investing?**

    A Discipline is essential in cryptocurrency investing as it helps investors stick to their trading plan, avoid emotional decision-making, and maintain a long-term perspective despite market fluctuations.

Q How can investors effectively manage the psychological pressures of trading in the cryptocurrency market?

   A Investors can manage psychological pressures by practising stress management techniques such as mindfulness meditation, regular exercise, setting boundaries for trading hours, and ensuring sufficient downtime to prevent burnout.

Q Why is it important for cryptocurrency investors to understand and manage emotional biases?

   A Understanding and managing emotional biases is crucial for investors to make rational decisions, avoid impulsive actions driven by emotions, and maintain a balanced approach to trading in the volatile cryptocurrency market.

Chapter 23

Holistic Cryptocurrency Investment Approach

Trading Plan & Strategy

Investors should craft a trading plan including entry and exit strategies and risk management techniques like stop-loss orders.

Utilising charting tools available on major crypto exchanges or platforms like TradingView is advisable. Investors should train themselves on indicators such as RSI, Stochastic, and MACD, which are crucial to gaining insight into each cryptocurrency's past and potential movement.

It is important to review the investment portfolio and market trends regularly. Being prepared to adjust the strategy based on new information or changes in an investor's financial situation is essential. Staying informed about market news, technological advancements, and regulatory developments that could impact one's investments is also recommended.

Emotional Discipline and Patience

The cryptocurrency market can be emotionally taxing for investors. Avoid making impulsive decisions based on short-term market movements. Instead, sticking to the investment plan and remembering that patience often pays off in the world of cryptocurrency investing is beneficial.

Lifestyle Considerations

Cryptocurrency investors should remember to balance their investment activities with their lifestyle, ensuring that their investments do not have a negative impact on their personal or professional lives.

Harnessing Artificial Intelligence for Enhanced Cryptocurrency Investing

Artificial intelligence (AI) significantly enhances cryptocurrency investing through advanced analytics and automation tools. AI algorithms can analyse large volumes of data, identify patterns, and generate trading signals to assist investors in making informed decisions.

Beginner investors can utilise AI tools for market analysis, risk management, and portfolio optimisation, while experienced traders can employ AI to automate trading strategies and execute trades more efficiently.

For instance, AI-powered trading bots can execute trades based on predefined criteria, reducing emotional bias and enhancing trading efficiency. By integrating AI and API tools into their investment strategies, investors can gain a competitive edge in the cryptocurrency market and achieve better investment outcomes.

Conclusion

Adopting a holistic approach to cryptocurrency investing is crucial for achieving long-term success in this dynamic and rapidly evolving market. By crafting a comprehensive trading plan, incorporating risk management strategies, and maintaining emotional discipline, investors can more effectively navigate the volatility of the crypto space.

Equally important is balancing investment activities with lifestyle considerations. It's crucial to ensure that one's crypto endeavours do not negatively impact personal or professional well-being, as this balance is key to sustaining a healthy and sustainable investment journey.

Furthermore, the strategic integration of emerging technologies, such as artificial intelligence, can provide investors with enhanced data-driven insights, improved trading efficiency, and a competitive edge in the cryptocurrency market. Leveraging these innovative tools can help investors make more informed decisions and capitalise on market opportunities.

The cryptocurrency sector is rapidly evolving, driven by significant technological advancements and an expanding range of applications. Staying informed about these developments is not just important but essential for investors to navigate the market effectively and identify lucrative investment opportunities.

Questions & Answers

Q **What is the significance of developing a trading plan and strategy in cryptocurrency investments?**

    A Developing a trading plan and strategy helps investors set clear goals, establish entry and exit points, manage risk effectively, and stay focused on long-term objectives in the dynamic cryptocurrency market.

Q **How do emotional discipline and patience contribute to successful cryptocurrency investing?**

    A Emotional discipline and patience enable investors to maintain a rational mindset, avoid impulsive decisions, and stay committed to their investment strategies, leading to better risk management and overall performance.

Q **Why should cryptocurrency investors consider lifestyle considerations in their investment approach?**

    A Considering lifestyle factors ensures that investments align with personal goals, values, and well-being, promoting a balanced approach to wealth management and sustainable investment practices.

Q **How can harnessing artificial intelligence enhance cryptocurrency investing?**

    A Harnessing artificial intelligence tools for market analysis, risk management, and automation can provide investors with data-driven insights, efficiency in trading operations, and a competitive edge in the cryptocurrency market.

Q **Why is continuous learning important for cryptocurrency investors?**

    A Continuous learning allows investors to stay updated on market trends, technological advancements, and regulatory changes, improving decision-making, adapting to evolving market conditions, and enhancing long-term investment success.

Chapter 24

Investment Exit Strategies for Cryptocurrency Investors

Planning and Risk Management

Cryptocurrency investors must develop effective exit strategies to maximise their gains and minimise losses in a highly volatile market. An exit strategy is a pre-planned approach to selling investments to achieve optimal returns or cut potential losses. This section explores various exit strategies tailored for cryptocurrency investments, which can help investors make informed decisions and manage risks effectively.

Understanding the Importance of Exit Strategies

An exit strategy is essential for managing investment risk and securing profits in the dynamic cryptocurrency market. Without a clear exit plan, investors might hold onto assets too long, potentially miss peak valuation periods, or panic sell during market downturns, leading to substantial losses.

Types of Exit Strategies for Cryptocurrency Investments

1. **Target Selling**: A popular cryptocurrency investment strategy involves setting specific price targets. A predetermined portion of the holdings is sold when these targets are achieved. This allows investors to gradually secure profits while keeping some exposure to potential future price increases. Multiple targets can be set to ensure a progressive profit-taking approach.

2. **Percentage Stop-Loss**: Implementing a stop-loss order at a certain percentage below the purchase price can limit losses. This strategy is particularly useful in managing downside risk without constantly monitoring the market. Due to cryptocurrencies' inherent volatility, wider stop-loss margins might be necessary.

3. **Trailing Stop-Loss**: A trailing stop-loss differs from a fixed stop-loss in that it protects profits by allowing a position to stay open and continue to profit as long as the price moves favourably. The stop-loss is adjusted dynamically and remains far from the current market price.

4. **Time-Based Exits**: Investors sometimes choose to exit their positions based on a predetermined time frame. For example, an investor may decide to hold onto a cryptocurrency for a specific duration, after which they plan to sell, regardless of the current market conditions. This approach can help avoid emotional biases from holding onto assets for too long.

5. **Fundamental Exit**: If significant modifications occur within a cryptocurrency venture or the broader market surroundings that adversely impact the initial investment rationale, it may be wise to withdraw from the investment. Such changes may include technological modifications, regulatory revisions, or market trends.

Developing a Personalised Exit Strategy

1. **Set Clear Goals**: Investors should determine their cryptocurrency investment goals, such as short-term gains or long-term growth, to determine their exit strategy.

2. **Assess Market Conditions**: It is important to stay updated on market trends and use technical analysis tools to make informed decisions about entering or exiting trades. Additionally, it is advisable to keep track of global economic factors that could impact the cryptocurrency market.

3. **Diversify the Portfolio**: Investing in various cryptocurrencies diversifies risks and allows for tailored exit strategies based on asset performance and risk profiles.

4. **Regularly Review and Adjust**: An effective exit strategy requires regular evaluation and flexibility to adapt to market conditions or investment goals. Regularly reviewing and making necessary adjustments is essential.

5. **Utilise Technology**: Leveraging trading platforms and tools that can automate exit strategies is recommended. Setting up automated sell orders based on set criteria can help execute exit strategies efficiently and remove emotional biases.

Conclusion

It is crucial for successful cryptocurrency investing to develop and implement a well-thought-out exit strategy. By doing so, investors can control their financial outcomes, secure their profits, and minimise potential losses. As the market continues to evolve, staying well-informed and adaptable will be key to effectively navigating the complexities of cryptocurrency investments.

Questions & Answers

Q Why is understanding the importance of exit strategies crucial for cryptocurrency investors?

A Understanding the importance of exit strategies helps investors manage risk, secure profits, and make informed decisions about when to sell their cryptocurrency investments for optimal returns.

Q What are the different types of exit strategies available for cryptocurrency investments?

A Different types of exit strategies include target selling, stop-loss orders, trailing stop orders, time-based exits, and fundamental exits, each tailored to specific investment goals and market conditions.

Q How can cryptocurrency investors develop a personalised exit strategy?

A Developing a personalised exit strategy involves setting clear goals, assessing market conditions, diversifying the portfolio, regularly reviewing and adjusting the strategy, and leveraging technology for automated execution, ensuring a tailored approach to exiting investments.

Chapter 25

Emerging Trends and Technologies in the Cryptocurrency Sector

Decentralised Autonomous Organisations (DAOs)

Decentralised Autonomous Organisations (DAOs) are a revolutionary concept in the world of cryptocurrency governance. These organisations operate on blockchain technology and rely on smart contracts to automate decision-making and operations. This eliminates the need for traditional hierarchical management structures and enables a community-driven approach to governance.

DAOs allow stakeholders to vote on key decisions and initiatives, making the decision-making process more transparent and democratic. As decentralised governance continues to evolve, DAOs could play a significant role in shaping the future of corporate and organisational governance.

Non-Fungible Tokens (NFTs)

The rise of non-fungible tokens (NFTs) has revolutionised the concept of digital ownership and asset tokenisation. These tokens allow for the unique representation of assets on the blockchain, which enables the verification of ownership and provenance of both digital and real-world assets.

This technology has particularly impacted the art and entertainment industries, allowing artists and creators to monetise their work in new ways while ensuring that ownership rights are preserved and protected.

For investors, NFTs represent a new asset class with the potential for significant returns, particularly as markets for digital goods and virtual assets continue to expand.

Blockchain Integration Across Industries

Blockchain technology is being integrated into various sectors, ranging from finance and healthcare to supply chain management and government operations. This integration highlights the technology's potential to improve transparency, efficiency, and security in traditional business processes. For instance, blockchain can offer immutable records of product origins, handling, and transportation in supply chain management, enhancing traceability and reducing fraud.

Investors interested in the broader application of blockchain technology should keep an eye on developments in these sectors as they present opportunities for innovative start-ups and established companies willing to integrate new technologies.

Innovations in Smart Contracts

The tech community has made significant progress in smart contract technology, pushing the limits of what can be automated on blockchain networks. Recent innovations include the development of more secure and flexible programming languages, improved handling of complex transactions and better user interfaces.

These advancements have opened up new potential use cases for smart contracts, ranging from complex financial instruments to automated legal agreements and beyond. For investors, these developments signify new opportunities in sectors that rely heavily on contractual agreements and transactions.

Future Outlook and Investment Opportunities

Analysing the latest trends and technologies in the cryptocurrency market is vital to identifying potential investment opportunities. As the industry continues to mature, areas such as decentralised finance (DeFi), tokenisation of real-world assets, and the convergence of AI with blockchain are expected to drive innovation and investment.

Staying up-to-date with these trends will help investors make informed decisions and take advantage of early-stage opportunities before they become mainstream.

Conclusion

The cryptocurrency sector is rapidly evolving, driven by the emergence of innovative technologies and the integration of blockchain across various industries. Decentralised Autonomous Organisations (DAOs), Non-Fungible Tokens (NFTs), and the convergence of blockchain with AI present exciting new investment opportunities for savvy investors.

By staying informed about these emerging trends and developments, investors can position themselves to capitalise on the growth potential of the cryptocurrency market. Continuous learning and adaptability will be crucial as the cryptocurrency landscape continues to evolve. By embracing these emerging trends and technologies, investors can unlock new avenues for growth and diversification within their cryptocurrency portfolios, positioning themselves for long-term success in this dynamic and rapidly advancing market.

Questions & Answers

Q What are Decentralised Autonomous Organisations (DAOs) and their significance in the cryptocurrency industry?

    A DAOs are organisations that operate autonomously on blockchain technology, enabling decentralised decision-making and governance. Understanding DAOs is crucial for investors to grasp the potential of community-driven projects in cryptocurrency.

Q How do Non-Fungible Tokens (NFTs) impact the cryptocurrency sector, and why are they important?

    A NFTs are unique digital assets representing ownership of digital or physical items. Exploring NFTs provides insights into the growing trend of digital ownership, art, collectibles, and tokenisation, offering new investment opportunities in the cryptocurrency market.

Q Why is blockchain integration across industries significant for the future of cryptocurrencies?

    A Blockchain integration across industries enhances transparency, security, and efficiency in various sectors like supply chain, finance, healthcare, and more. Understanding this trend helps investors identify potential use cases and investment opportunities in blockchain technology.

Q What are the innovations in smart contracts, and what are their implications for cryptocurrency investors?

    A Innovations in smart contracts enable self-executing agreements on the blockchain, revolutionising processes like automated transactions, decentralised finance, and governance. Exploring smart contract advancements provides insights into the evolving landscape of cryptocurrency investments.

Q How can investors benefit from understanding the future outlook and investment opportunities in the cryptocurrency sector?

A Understanding the future outlook and investment opportunities in the cryptocurrency sector helps investors anticipate trends, identify emerging technologies, and position themselves for potential growth and success in the dynamic and evolving cryptocurrency market.

Closing Remarks

The cryptocurrency sector has emerged as a dynamic and rapidly evolving landscape, driven by significant advancements in blockchain technology and the expanding applications of digital assets. As this market continues to mature, staying informed about the latest developments, trends, and investment opportunities is not only essential but also holds the promise of long-term success for investors who navigate this space effectively, keeping them engaged and proactive in their investment journey.

This comprehensive guide has provided a robust framework to help novice and experienced investors make well-informed decisions aligned with their financial objectives and risk tolerance. By exploring the core concepts of cryptocurrencies, setting clear investment goals, and implementing effective portfolio management strategies, investors can lay the foundation for a rewarding crypto investment journey.

A crucial aspect highlighted throughout this handbook is the role of diversification in mitigating risks and enhancing the resilience of investment portfolios. By allocating investments across various digital assets, investors can diversify their exposure and unlock new opportunities.

Navigating the volatile cryptocurrency market also requires a disciplined and strategic approach to risk management. Implementing techniques like stop-loss orders, managing leverage, and learning from real-world case studies can help investors protect their capital and optimise their returns.

Recognising the significance of security and regulatory compliance, this guide has offered detailed guidance on selecting reputable exchanges, managing personal wallets, and staying up-to-date with the evolving regulatory landscape. By prioritising these aspects, investors can safeguard their assets and ensure their activities align with the legal and ethical standards of the industry.

Beyond technical and financial considerations, this handbook has also emphasised the importance of understanding and managing emotional biases in the investment process. Investors can significantly enhance their decision-making process and long-term success by maintaining discipline and patience and employing effective stress management strategies.

As the cryptocurrency sector continues to evolve, investors who embrace a holistic approach, combining technical expertise, risk management, and a commitment to continuous learning, will be well-positioned to navigate the market's complexities and capitalise on emerging opportunities. By following the strategies and insights outlined in this guide, investors can feel empowered, confident, and in control of their ability to achieve their financial goals and contribute to the sustainable growth of the cryptocurrency ecosystem.

Glossary of Terms

1. **All-Time High (ATH)**: Represents the highest price level a cryptocurrency has ever reached, often triggering psychological challenges for investors.

2. **AML/KYC Compliance:** Anti-Money Laundering (AML) and Know Your Customer (KYC) regulations that require cryptocurrency businesses to verify the identity of their customers and report suspicious activities to prevent financial crimes.

3. **Artificial Intelligence (AI):** The simulation of human intelligence processes by machines, such as computer algorithms, to analyse data, make predictions, and automate tasks in cryptocurrency investing.

4. **Asset Classes:** Different categories of investments, such as stocks, bonds, and real estate, that have unique characteristics and risk-return profiles.

5. **Bear Market:** A market condition where asset prices are falling, typically characterised by investor pessimism and sustained downward trends.

6. **Bitcoin:** The first and most famous cryptocurrency created by Satoshi Nakamoto in 2008. Bitcoin uses blockchain to enable peer-to-peer transactions without the need for intermediaries like banks.

7. **Blockchain:** A decentralised, distributed ledger technology that records transactions across multiple computers in a secure and transparent manner. Each block in the chain contains a cryptographic hash of the previous block, creating a secure and immutable record.

8. **Bollinger Bands:** A technical analysis tool that consists of a set of lines plotted two standard deviations away from a simple moving

average. Bollinger Bands help traders identify volatility and potential price breakouts.

9. **Borrowing Fee**: The interest charged by exchanges or brokers for borrowing assets in short-selling.

10. **Bubble**: A market phenomenon characterised by a rapid escalation of asset prices followed by a sudden and significant decline. This is often driven by speculative excess and investor psychology.

11. **Bull Market:** A market condition where asset prices are rising, typically characterised by investor optimism and sustained upward trends.

12. **Candlestick Patterns:** Visual representations of price movements in financial markets, used in technical analysis to predict future price movements.

13. **Confirmation Bias**: Refers to the tendency to search for, interpret, or remember information in a way that confirms one's preexisting beliefs or hypotheses. This could lead to biased decision-making.

14. **Centralised Exchanges:** Traditional cryptocurrency trading platforms that operate with a central authority to facilitate transactions between buyers and sellers.

15. **Coins vs. Tokens: Coins** are Cryptocurrencies that operate on their own blockchain, such as Bitcoin and Ethereum, and serve as a form of digital currency for transactions within their respective networks. **Tokens** are Digital assets built on existing blockchains, like ERC-20 tokens on the Ethereum network, representing assets, utility, or ownership in a project or ecosystem.

16. **Cold Storage:** A method of storing cryptocurrencies offline in hardware wallets or paper wallets to protect them from online hacking attempts.

17. **Community Engagement:** Involvement and interaction with the cryptocurrency community to gain insights, share knowledge, and stay informed about market trends and developments.

18. **Compliance:** Adherence to regulatory requirements and standards, such as Anti-Money Laundering (AML) and Know Your Customer (KYC) regulations, to ensure legal and ethical practices in the cryptocurrency industry.

19. **Continuous Learning:** The ongoing process of acquiring new knowledge and skills in the cryptocurrency industry to stay informed about market trends, technological advancements, and investment opportunities.

20. **Correlations:** The degree to which two or more assets move in relation to each other. Understanding correlations helps investors diversify their portfolios and manage risk effectively.

21. **Crypto Investment:** The act of investing in cryptocurrencies or digital assets with the aim of generating returns. It involves buying, holding, or trading digital currencies for profit.

22. **Cryptocurrencies:** Digital or virtual currencies that use cryptography for security and operate independently of central authorities like governments or banks.

23. **Cryptocurrency ETFs:** Exchange-Traded Funds (ETFs) that track the performance of cryptocurrencies or blockchain-related assets. They provide investors with exposure to the cryptocurrency market without directly owning digital assets.

24. **Cryptocurrency Exchanges:** Platforms where users can buy, sell, and trade cryptocurrencies with other users, providing liquidity and price discovery.

25. **Cryptocurrency Mining:** The process of validating transactions and adding them to the blockchain through computational power, typically rewarded with new coins.

26. **Cryptocurrency Wallets:** Digital wallets that store private keys used to access and manage cryptocurrencies, available in various forms like hardware, software, and paper.

27. **Cryptography**: The practice and study of techniques for securing digital information, communication, and computation. Cryptography is a fundamental component of blockchain technology, ensuring the integrity and security of cryptocurrency transactions.

28. **Decentralisation:** The distribution of control and decision-making across a network of participants, rather than being centralised in a single entity. Decentralisation is a key principle in cryptocurrencies and blockchain technology.

29. **Decentralised Autonomous Organisations (DAOs)**: Organisations governed by smart contracts and run on blockchain technology. DAOs operate without a central authority and allow members to vote on decisions using tokens.

30. **DeFi (Decentralised Finance):** Financial services built on blockchain technology that aim to decentralise and democratise traditional finance, offering services like lending, borrowing, and trading.

31. **Discipline**: Refers to adhering to a predetermined trading plan, following established rules, and maintaining a consistent approach to investing despite emotional impulses or market fluctuations.

32. **Diversification:** Spreading investments across different assets to reduce risk by not putting all eggs in one basket.

33. **Emotional Biases**: Psychological factors that can influence investor behaviour and decision-making in financial markets, leading to irrational or emotionally driven investment choices.

34. **Environmental Impact:** The effect of cryptocurrency mining on the environment, including energy consumption and carbon footprint.

35. **Ethereum:** A blockchain platform that enables the creation of smart contracts and decentralised applications (dApps), known for its programmability and flexibility.

36. **Exit Strategy:** A plan outlining how an investor will exit or liquidate their investments in cryptocurrencies. Exit strategies help investors manage risk and lock in profits.

37. **Fear of Missing Out (FOMO)**: A psychological bias that drives investors to make impulsive decisions. It is based on the fear of missing out on potential gains in a rapidly rising market.

38. **Fear, Uncertainty, and Doubt (FUD)**: A common phenomenon in the cryptocurrency market. Negative information or rumours create fear and uncertainty among investors, leading to panic selling and market downturns.

39. **Fiat**: In the context of cryptocurrency, "fiat" refers to government-issued currency that is not backed by a physical commodity such as gold or silver but rather by the government that issued it. Examples include the U.S. Dollar (USD), Euro (EUR), and Japanese Yen (JPY). Fiat currencies are used as the standard medium of exchange for goods and services and are often used to purchase cryptocurrencies on exchanges.

40. **Fundamental Analysis:** An approach to evaluating investments by analysing financial statements, economic indicators, and other qualitative and quantitative factors. Fundamental analysis aims to determine the intrinsic value of an asset.

41. **Future Outlook:** Predictions and analysis of potential trends, developments, and opportunities in the cryptocurrency sector based on technological advancements, market dynamics, and regulatory changes.

42. **Global Economic Factors:** Economic conditions, policies, and events that impact the cryptocurrency market, such as interest rates, inflation, geopolitical tensions, and regulatory changes.

43. **Greed**: A psychological bias that can drive investors to take excessive risks or pursue unrealistic returns in the pursuit of profit.

44. **Hardware Wallets:** Physical devices that securely store private keys offline, providing enhanced security for cryptocurrency holdings.

45. **Impermanent Loss:** A temporary loss experienced by liquidity providers in automated market-making protocols. Impermanent loss occurs when the price of the assets in a liquidity pool changes relative to when they were deposited.

46. **Initial Coin Offering (ICO):** A fundraising method used by blockchain projects to raise capital by issuing tokens to investors. ICOs are a way for companies to crowdfund their projects by selling digital tokens.

47. **Initial Exchange Offering (IEO)**: A way to raise funds in the cryptocurrency space by conducting a token sale on a cryptocurrency exchange platform. Unlike Initial Coin Offerings (ICOs), which are directly conducted by the project team, IEOs are facilitated by exchanges. This provides a more secure and streamlined process for token sales. Investors can participate in IEOs through the exchange's platform, which offers a high level of trust and convenience when acquiring new tokens, making the process more secure.

48. **Innovations in Smart Contracts:** Advancements in blockchain technology that enable self-executing agreements, automated transactions, and decentralised governance in the cryptocurrency space.

49. **Inter-Market Analysis:** Analysing the relationships between different markets, such as cryptocurrencies and traditional financial instruments, to identify correlations and trading opportunities.

50. **Interim Loss:** A temporary loss experienced by liquidity providers in decentralised finance (DeFi) platforms due to price fluctuations in the assets held in a liquidity pool.

51. **Investment Goals:** Objectives set by investors to achieve specific financial outcomes through their cryptocurrency investments.

52. **Investment Opportunities:** Potential avenues for generating returns and diversifying portfolios in the cryptocurrency market, such as emerging technologies, decentralised applications, and innovative projects.

53. **Investor Psychology:** The study of how psychological factors influence investor behaviour and decision-making in financial markets.

54. **Leverage**: The use of borrowed capital to increase the potential return of an investment.

55. **Lifestyle Considerations:** Personal factors, such as risk tolerance, financial goals, and time commitment, that influence an individual's investment decisions and trading strategies.

56. **Loss Aversion**: The psychological tendency for individuals to prefer avoiding losses over acquiring equivalent gains. This often results in risk-averse behaviour in investment decisions.

57. **Limit Orders:** Orders to buy or sell a cryptocurrency at a specific price or better. Limit orders are executed only when the market reaches the specified price.

58. **Liquidation**: The forced closing of a trading position when the losses reach a certain threshold, typically in margin trading.

59. **Liquidity Pool:** A pool of funds locked in a decentralised finance (DeFi) platform to facilitate trading and provide liquidity for users. Liquidity pools enable users to trade assets without relying on traditional order books.

60. **Liquidity:** The ease with which an asset can be bought or sold in the market without significantly impacting its price. High liquidity indicates a large number of buyers and sellers, making it easier to trade an asset.

61. **MACD (Moving Average Convergence Divergence):** A popular technical analysis indicator that measures the relationship between two moving averages of an asset's price. MACD is used to identify trend reversals and potential buy or sell signals.

62. **Margin Call:** A demand from a broker that an investor deposit additional money or securities into their account when the account value falls below a certain threshold.

63. **Margin Trading:** Trading with borrowed funds to increase potential profits, but also increasing potential losses.

64. **Market Analysis:** Evaluation of market trends, price movements, and other factors to make informed decisions in cryptocurrency trading and investing.

65. **Market Capitalisation:** The total value of a cryptocurrency in circulation, calculated by multiplying the current price by the total supply of coins or tokens. Market capitalisation is used to rank cryptocurrencies by size.

66. **Market Manipulation:** The deliberate attempt to interfere with a market's free and fair operation. This is often done through fraudulent activities or deceptive practices to influence asset prices.

67. **Market Orders:** Orders to buy or sell a cryptocurrency at the current market price. Market orders are executed immediately at the best available price.

68. **Market Volatility:** The degree of variation in the price of an asset over time. Cryptocurrency markets are known for their high volatility, which can lead to significant price fluctuations.

69. **Moving Averages:** A technical analysis tool that smooths out price data by creating a constantly updated average price. Moving averages help traders identify trends and potential entry or exit points.

70. **Multi-Market Analysis:** Analysing different but related markets to assess the strength or weakness of a cryptocurrency. Multi-market analysis helps investors understand the broader economic factors influencing asset prices.

71. **Multi-Signature Wallet:** A cryptocurrency wallet that requires multiple private keys to authorise transactions. Multi-signature wallets enhance security by requiring multiple approvals for fund transfers.

72. **Non-Fungible Tokens (NFTs):** Unique digital assets that represent ownership of a specific item or piece of content, often used in art, collectibles, and gaming. NFTs are indivisible and cannot be exchanged on a like-for-like basis.

73. **OTC Trading:** Over-the-Counter trading, a method of trading cryptocurrencies directly between two parties without the need for a centralised exchange. OTC trading is often used for large transactions or illiquid assets.

74. **Pairs Trading:** A trading strategy that involves taking opposite positions in two correlated assets.

75. **Panic Buying**: The opposite of panic selling, where investors rush to buy assets frenzied or irrationally. This is often driven by fear of missing out or speculative hype.

76. **Panic Selling**: Selling assets when a person is distressed or emotional due to fear, uncertainty, or market volatility. This often leads to significant price declines.

77. **Phishing:** A deceptive practice where cybercriminals impersonate legitimate sources to trick individuals into revealing sensitive information like passwords and financial data. These fraudulent attempts, often through emails or websites, can lead to identity theft and economic harm. Vigilance is the key to protecting personal information and digital assets.

78. **Portfolio Management:** The art and science of managing a collection of investments, known as a portfolio, to achieve specific financial goals. Diversification and asset allocation are key components of portfolio management.

79. **Proof of Stake (PoS)**: A consensus mechanism used by some blockchain networks, where validators are selected to add new blocks to the chain based on the amount of cryptocurrency they hold (their "stake") rather than computational power. PoS aims to be more energy-efficient than the Proof of Work (PoW) consensus.

80. **Proof of Work (PoW)**: A consensus mechanism used by some blockchain networks, where miners compete to solve complex mathematical problems to validate transactions and add new blocks to the chain. The miner who solves the problem first is rewarded with new cryptocurrency. PoW is energy-intensive but provides a secure way to maintain the blockchain.

81. **Prospectus:** A legal document provided by an investment fund or ETF that discloses essential information about the fund, including its investment objectives, risks, fees, and performance.

82. **Read-Only Wallet:** A type of cryptocurrency wallet that allows users to view their balances and transactions without the ability to send or receive funds. Read-only wallets provide enhanced security for monitoring purposes.

83. **Recovery Phrase:** A series of words generated during the setup of a cryptocurrency wallet that serves as a backup to recover the wallet and funds in case of loss or damage to the device.

84. **Regulatory Compliance:** Adhering to laws, regulations, and industry standards governing the operation of cryptocurrency businesses and investments. Compliance with regulations helps ensure transparency, security, and legality in the crypto space.

85. **Risk Management:** The process of identifying, assessing, and mitigating risks associated with investments. Effective risk management strategies help investors protect their capital and minimise losses.

86. **RSI (Relative Strength Index):** An oscillator indicator used in technical analysis to measure the speed and change of price movements. RSI helps investors identify overbought or oversold conditions in the market.

87. **Security Measures:** Precautions and protocols implemented to safeguard cryptocurrency holdings and transactions from unauthorised access, theft, or hacking.

88. **Security Tokens:** Digital tokens that represent ownership of real-world assets, such as equity in a company or ownership of physical assets. Security tokens are subject to securities regulations.

89. **Sentiment Analysis:** The process of analysing market sentiment or investor emotions to gauge the overall attitude towards a particular cryptocurrency or asset. Sentiment analysis helps investors understand market trends and potential price movements.

90. **Short-Selling**: A trading strategy where an investor borrows an asset, sells it at the current market price, and aims to buy it back later at a lower price to profit from the price difference.

91. **Short Squeeze**: A rapid increase in the price of an asset that forces short sellers to close their positions, often leading to further price increases.

92. **Smart Contracts:** Self-executing contracts with predefined rules and conditions written in code on blockchain platforms like Ethereum, automating and enforcing agreements.

93. **Staking:** The process of participating in a Proof-of-Stake (PoS) blockchain network by holding and locking up a certain amount of cryptocurrency to support network operations. Stakers are rewarded with additional coins for their participation.

94. **Stop-Loss Orders:** Orders set by traders to automatically sell a cryptocurrency at a predetermined price to limit losses and manage risk in volatile markets.

95. **Support and Resistance Levels:** Key price levels where a cryptocurrency's price tends to find support (price stops falling) or resistance (price stops rising). Support and resistance levels are used by traders to make trading decisions.

96. **Taxation Considerations:** The tax implications of buying, selling, and holding cryptocurrencies. Understanding tax laws and reporting requirements is essential for cryptocurrency investors to comply with tax regulations.

97. **Technical Analysis:** Analysis of historical price data and trading volumes to forecast future price movements and make trading decisions based on chart patterns and indicators.

98. **Tokenomics:** The economic model and principles governing the creation, distribution, and management of tokens within a blockchain ecosystem.

99. **Trading Indicators:** Tools and metrics used in technical analysis to interpret price data and identify potential buy or sell signals in cryptocurrency trading.

100. **Trading Volume:** The total amount of a cryptocurrency traded within a specific period, usually hours. Trading volume indicates the liquidity and interest in a particular asset.

101. **Trading:** The buying and selling of financial instruments, such as cryptocurrencies, stocks, or commodities, with the goal of making a profit from price fluctuations.

102. **Utility Tokens**: Tokens that provide access to a specific product or service within a blockchain-based platform or ecosystem. Utility tokens are designed to have a practical use case rather than solely for investment purposes.

103. **Whitepaper:** A document outlining the technical details, purpose, and features of a blockchain project or cryptocurrency. Whitepapers are used to communicate the project's vision and technology to potential investors and users.

104. **Yield Farming:** A strategy in DeFi where investors provide liquidity to decentralised platforms in exchange for rewards, such as interest or additional tokens. Yield farming aims to maximise returns on cryptocurrency holdings.

Interactive Quizzes (Questions)

Cryptocurrency investors are invited to explore the Interactive Quizzes section, designed specifically for them to test their understanding of key concepts from each chapter. This section presents thought-provoking questions and insightful answers to help evaluate comprehension and reinforce learning about cryptocurrency investments.

To create an optimal learning experience, questions and answers are presented on separate pages. This enables readers to engage with the questions first, without the distraction of the immediate answers, allowing for an independent assessment of knowledge before verification.

How to Use the Interactive Quizzes:

1. **Carefully Review the Questions**: Assess your grasp of the chapter content.

2. **Challenge Yourself**: Attempt to answer each question to the best of your ability before checking the provided answers.

3. **Self-Assessment Tool**: Utilise the quizzes to gauge understanding and identify areas that may require further exploration.

4. **Revisit Chapter Material**: Reinforce knowledge by revisiting the chapter material and improving performance in the quizzes.

5. **Engage in Interactive Learning**: Immerse yourself in an interactive learning experience and enjoy testing your expertise in cryptocurrency investments.

Embark on an educational journey through the Interactive Quizzes section, designed to assess your knowledge and deepen your understanding of cryptocurrency investments. Good luck with your quiz endeavours!

1. Understanding the Basics:

a. **Multiple Choice Question**: What is the core philosophy of decentralisation in cryptocurrencies? A) Centralised control B) Distributed governance C) Peer-to-peer transactions D) Community

b. **True or False**: Understanding the basics of cryptocurrencies is not essential for making informed investment decisions. (True/False)

c. **Fill in the Blank**: Coins and tokens differ in their _____.

2. Setting the Investment Goals:

a. **Scenario-Based Question**: Why is calculating the investment amount important in setting investment goals?

b. **True or False**: Short-term investing involves holding assets for an extended period to maximise returns. (True/False)

c. **Fill in the Blank**: Defining the investment horizon helps investors tailor strategies to match their financial goals, risk tolerance, and _____.

3. Portfolio Management and Diversification:

a. **Multiple Choice Question**: What is one criterion for diversifying a crypto portfolio? A) Investing in a single asset B) Focusing on short-term gains C) Spreading investments across different assets D) Ignoring risk management

b. **True or False**: Implementing a diversification strategy in a crypto portfolio helps minimise risks. (True/False)

c. **Fill in the Blank**: Diversification in cryptocurrency portfolios helps reduce exposure to _____.

4. Environmental Impact of Cryptocurrency Mining

a. **Multiple Choice Question**: What is one innovation in mining technology to reduce the environmental impact? A) Increased energy consumption B) Shift towards renewable energy C) Higher carbon emissions D) Decreased transparency

    b. **True or False**: Regulatory influence has no impact on the environmental practices of cryptocurrency mining. (True/False)

    c. **Fill in the Blank**: The role of community and transparency is crucial in mitigating the _____ of cryptocurrency mining.

5. Staking and Yield Farming:

    a. **Scenario-Based Question**: What are the benefits of yield farming in the cryptocurrency market?

    b. **True or False**: Staking involves securing networks and earning rewards by selling digital assets. (True/False)

    c. **Fill in the Blank**: Yield farming offers opportunities for investors to earn _____ in the cryptocurrency markets.

6. Understanding Cryptocurrency ETFs:

    a. **Multiple Choice Question**: What is an ETF in the context of cryptocurrencies? A) Electronic Trading Fund B) Exchange-Traded Fund C) Exclusive Token Fund D) Efficient Transaction Framework

    b. **True or False**: Investing in cryptocurrency ETFs does not require considerations before making investment decisions. (True/False)

    c. **Fill in the Blank**: Cryptocurrency ETFs provide benefits such as diversification and exposure to the crypto market without _____.

7. Risk Management Strategies:

    a. **Multiple Choice Question**: What is a key component of successful cryptocurrency investing? A) High volatility B) Impulsive decision-making C) Effective risk management D) Lack of diversification

b. **True or False**: Setting stop-loss orders is not a risk management strategy in cryptocurrency investing. (True/False)

c. **Fill in the Blank**: Diversification across asset classes helps investors spread risk and avoid _____.

8. Market Analysis Techniques for Cryptocurrency Investors:

a. **Scenario-Based Question**: How can sentiment analysis tools benefit cryptocurrency investors?

b. **True or False**: Technical analysis indicators are not useful for predicting market movements in cryptocurrencies. (True/False)

c. **Fill in the Blank**: Practical application of market analysis involves using tools to interpret market data and make _____ decisions.

9. Choosing the Right Cryptocurrencies:

a. **Multiple Choice Question**: What is a key factor to consider when identifying leading cryptocurrencies? A) Market volatility B) Community support C) Regulatory restrictions D) Lack of transparency

b. **True or False**: Daily traded volumes are not indicative of liquidity and investor interest in cryptocurrencies. (True/False)

c. **Fill in the Blank**: Industry insights and trends provide valuable information on market dynamics and emerging _____.

10. Understanding Crypto Indexes:

a. **Multiple Choice**: Which of the following is NOT a common type of crypto index? A) Market-cap-weighted index B) Equal-weighted index C) Volatility-based index D) Sector-specific index

b. **True or False**: Crypto indexes can only be used for tracking market performance and cannot be directly invested in. (True/False)

c. **Fill in the Blank**: A _____ index includes cryptocurrencies from a specific sector within the crypto market, such as DeFi or privacy coins.

11. Introduction to Short-Selling Cryptocurrencies:

a. **Scenario-Based Question**: How can short-selling be used as a hedging strategy in cryptocurrency investing?

b. **True or False**: In short-selling, potential profits are unlimited while losses are limited. (True/False)

c. **Fill in the Blank**: Short-selling involves borrowing an asset, selling it, and then _____ it at a lower price to profit from price declines.

12. Decentralised Finance vs. Centralised Exchanges for Trading:

a. **Multiple Choice Question**: What is a key advantage of using decentralised finance (DeFi) platforms over centralised exchanges? A) Higher liquidity B) User control of funds C) Limited financial products D) Fiat integration

b. **True or False**: Centralised exchanges offer complete control over user funds, similar to DeFi platforms. (True/False)

c. **Fill in the Blank**: Decentralised finance platforms provide opportunities for users to earn passive income through _____.

13. Case Studies on Successful Investments in Cryptocurrency:

a. **Scenario-Based Question**: What can investors learn from the success of early Bitcoin investors?

b. **True or False**: Binance Coin (BNB) is not a successful case study in cryptocurrency investments. (True/False)

c. **Fill in the Blank**: The Link Marine Community and Chainlink exemplify the power of _____ in cryptocurrency success stories.

14. Analysis and Advanced Trading Strategies:

a. **Multiple Choice Question**: What is a key benefit of over-the-counter (OTC) trading in cryptocurrency? A) Limited liquidity B) Lower fees C) Higher market impact D) Lack of privacy

b. **True or False**: Technical analysis tools are not useful for predicting market trends in cryptocurrency trading. (True/False)

c. **Fill in the Blank**: Advanced trading options on cryptocurrency exchanges provide investors with tools to enhance their trading strategies and _____.

15. Understanding Limit and Market Orders:

a. **Multiple Choice Question**: What is the primary difference between limit orders and market orders in cryptocurrency trading? A) Execution speed B) Price certainty C) Order type D) Order size

b. **True or False**: Market orders prioritise speed over price in cryptocurrency trading. (True/False)

c. **Fill in the Blank**: Strategic application of limit orders involves setting appropriate price levels to ensure _____ execution.

16. Security Measures, Exchanges, and Wallet Management:

a. **Scenario-Based Question**: Why is it recommended to transfer cryptocurrencies to personal wallets instead of keeping them on exchanges?

b. **True or False**: Hardware wallets are less secure than software wallets for storing cryptocurrencies. (True/False)

c. **Fill in the Blank**: Multi-signature support in wallets requires _____ approvals before making a transaction, enhancing security.

17. Regulatory Updates & Compliance in Crypto Investments:

a. **Multiple Choice Question**: What is a key aspect of AML/KYC compliance in cryptocurrency investments? A) Anonymity B) Identity verification C) Decentralisation D) High-frequency trading

b. **True or False**: Regulatory frameworks for cryptocurrencies are uniform across all countries. (True/False)

c. **Fill in the Blank**: Understanding the _____ landscape is crucial for cryptocurrency investors to ensure compliance and mitigate legal risks.

18. Regulatory Updates and Investment Insights for Stablecoins:

a. **Scenario-Based Question**: How does reserve management transparency affect stablecoin investments?

b. **True or False**: Central Bank Digital Currencies (CBDCs) have no impact on the stablecoin market. (True/False)

c. **Fill in the Blank**: Compliance with _____ regulations is essential for stablecoin issuers to maintain trust and stability.

19. Crypto-Friendly Banking and Payment Strategies:

a. **Multiple Choice Question**: What is a key consideration when dealing with crypto-friendly banks? A) Limited transaction options B) Regulatory compliance C) High fees D) Lack of security

b. **True or False**: Intermediary payment processors are not necessary for crypto transactions. (True/False)

c. **Fill in the Blank**: Examples of payment processors include _____ that facilitate crypto transactions.

20. Tax Planning Strategies for Cryptocurrency Investors:

a. **Multiple Choice Question**: Why is keeping detailed records of transactions essential for cryptocurrency investors? A) To avoid taxes B) To ensure compliance C) To increase profits D) To hide transactions

b. **True or False**: Utilising tax-loss harvesting involves intentionally selling assets at a loss to reduce tax liabilities. (True/False)

c. **Fill in the Blank**: Retirement accounts can provide cryptocurrency investors with opportunities for tax-_____ growth.

21. Community Engagement and Networking in the Crypto Space:

a. **Scenario-Based Question**: Why is community engagement important for cryptocurrency investors?

b. **True or False**: Collaborative learning and knowledge sharing are not beneficial for investors in the crypto community. (True/False)

c. **Fill in the Blank**: Building a network of investors can lead to valuable _____ opportunities and partnerships.

22. Psychology of Investing in Cryptocurrencies:

a. **Multiple Choice Question**: What is a key factor in managing emotional biases in cryptocurrency investing? A) Technical analysis B) Market trends C) Discipline D) Regulatory changes

b. **True or False**: Stress management techniques are not relevant for cryptocurrency investors. (True/False)

c. **Fill in the Blank**: Understanding investor psychology can help investors make _____ investment decisions.

23. Holistic Cryptocurrency Investment Approach:

a. **Multiple Choice Question**: What is a key component of a trading plan in cryptocurrency investing? A) Emotional bias B) Patience C) Risk management D) Market trends

b. **True or False**: Continuous learning is not necessary for success in cryptocurrency investing. (True/False)

c. **Fill in the Blank**: Harnessing artificial intelligence in cryptocurrency investing can lead to enhanced _____ outcomes.

24. Investment Exit Strategies for Cryptocurrency Investors:

a. **Scenario-Based Question**: Why is understanding the importance of exit strategies crucial for cryptocurrency investors?
b. **True or False**: There is only one type of exit strategy for cryptocurrency investments. (True/False)
c. **Fill in the Blank**: Developing a personalised exit strategy involves considering individual _____ and risk tolerance.

25. Emerging Trends and Technologies in the Cryptocurrency Sector:

a. **Multiple Choice Question**: What is a key innovation in the cryptocurrency sector? A) Traditional banking B) Centralised governance C) Decentralised Autonomous Organisations (DAOs) D) Closed-loop systems
b. **True or False**: Non-Fungible Tokens (NFTs) have no relevance in the cryptocurrency sector. (True/False)
c. **Fill in the Blank**: Understanding blockchain integration across industries can provide insights into _____ opportunities.

Interactive Quizzes (Answers)

1. Understanding the Basics:

a. Answer: **B) Distributed governance**
b. Answer: **False**
c. Answer: **Utility and purpose**

2. Setting the Investment Goals:

a. Answer: **Calculating the investment amount ensures that investments align with financial health and objectives**.
b. Answer: **False**
c. Answer: **Time available for managing portfolios**

3. Portfolio Management and Diversification:

a. Answer: **C) Spreading investments across different assets**
b. Answer: **True**
c. Answer: **Single asset risk**

4. Environmental Impact of Cryptocurrency Mining

a. Answer: **B) Shift towards renewable energy**
b. Answer: **False**
c. Answer: **Environmental impact**

5. Staking and Yield Farming:

a. Answer: **Yield farming allows investors to leverage crypto assets for higher returns through various DeFi protocols**.
b. Answer: **False**
c. Answer: **Passive income**

6. Understanding Cryptocurrency ETFs:

    a. Answer: **B) Exchange-Traded Fund**

    b. Answer: **False**

    c. Answer: **Direct ownership of digital assets**

7. Risk Management Strategies:

    a. Answer: **C) Effective risk management**

    b. Answer: **False**

    c. Answer: **Concentration risk**

8. Market Analysis Techniques for Cryptocurrency Investors:

    a. Answer: **Sentiment analysis tools help investors gauge market sentiment and make informed decisions based on crowd emotions.**

    b. Answer: **False**

    c. Answer: **Informed**

9. Choosing the Right Cryptocurrencies:

    a. Answer: **B) Community support**

    b. Answer: **False**

    c. Answer: **Technologies**

10. Understanding Crypto Indexes:

    a. Answer: **C) Volatility-based index. While volatility can be a factor in some index methodologies, it's not a common standalone type of crypto index, as described in the chapter.**

    b. Answer: **False**

    c. Answer: **Sector-specific**

11. Introduction to Short-Selling Cryptocurrencies:

a. Answer: **Short-selling can be used as a hedging strategy by allowing investors to profit from or offset potential losses in long positions during market downturns.**

b. Answer: **False**

c. Answer: **Buying back**

12. Decentralised Finance vs. Centralised Exchanges for Trading:

a. Answer: **B) User control of funds**

b. Answer: **False**

c. Answer: **Yield farming**

13. Case Studies on Successful Investments in Cryptocurrency:

a. Answer: **Early Bitcoin investors benefited from the long-term growth potential of the cryptocurrency, showcasing the importance of strategic investment decisions.**

b. Answer: **False**

c. Answer: **Community support**

14. Analysis and Advanced Trading Strategies:

a. Answer: **B) Lower fees**

b. Answer: **False**

c. Answer: **Improve outcomes**

15. Understanding Limit and Market Orders:

a. Answer: **B) Price certainty**

b. Answer: **True**

c. Answer: **Optimal**

16. Security Measures, Exchanges, and Wallet Management:

    a. Answer: **Transferring cryptocurrencies to personal wallets reduces the risk of loss due to exchange hacks and provides users with more control over their assets.**

    b. Answer: **False**

    c. Answer: **Multiple**

17. Regulatory Updates & Compliance in Crypto Investments:

    a. Answer: **B) Identity verification.**

    b. Answer: **False**

    c. Answer: **Regulatory**

18. Regulatory Updates and Investment Insights for Stablecoins:

    a. Answer: **Transparent reserve management increases investor confidence in stablecoins, potentially leading to higher adoption and stability in the market.**

    b. Answer: **False**

    c. Answer: **AML and KYC**

19. Crypto-Friendly Banking and Payment Strategies:

    a. Answer: **B) Regulatory compliance**

    b. Answer: **False**

    c. Answer: **Intermediaries**

20. Tax Planning Strategies for Cryptocurrency Investors:

    a. Answer: **B) To ensure compliance**

    b. Answer: **True**

    c. Answer: **Deferred**

21. Community Engagement and Networking in the Crypto Space:

   a. Answer: **Community engagement allows investors to stay informed, build relationships, and access valuable insights within the crypto space.**

   b. Answer: **False**

   c. Answer: **Collaboration**

22. Psychology of Investing in Cryptocurrencies:

   a. Answer: **C) Discipline**

   b. Answer: **False**

   c. Answer: **Informed**

23. Holistic Cryptocurrency Investment Approach:

   a. Answer: **C) Risk management**

   b. Answer: **False**

   c. Answer: **Investment**

24. Investment Exit Strategies for Cryptocurrency Investors:

   a. Answer: **Exit strategies help investors manage risk, lock in profits, and make informed decisions about when to sell their assets.**

   b. Answer: **False**

   c. Answer: **Goals**

25. Emerging Trends and Technologies in the Cryptocurrency Sector:

   a. Answer: **C) Decentralised Autonomous Organisations (DAOs)**

   b. Answer: **False**

   c. Answer: **Investment**

References

1. **Nakamoto, S. (2008).** Bitcoin: A Peer-to-Peer Electronic Cash System. https://bitcoin.org/bitcoin.pdf
2. **Buterin, V. (2013).** Ethereum: A Next-Generation Smart Contract and Decentralized Application Platform. https://ethereum.org/whitepaper/
3. **Binance Academy. (2024).** What is Binance Coin (BNB)? https://academy.binance.com/en/articles/what-is-bnb.
4. **Chainlink. (2022).** The Link Marine Community. https://chainlinktoday.com/thelinkmarine-inspires-chainlink-community-to-turn-their-ideas-into-reality/
5. **Solana. (2024).** Solana's Rapid Ascent. https://solana.com/ecosystem
6. **Investopedia. (2024).** Technical Analysis. https://www.investopedia.com/terms/t/technicalanalysis.asp
7. **Investopedia. (2023).** Fundamental Analysis. https://www.investopedia.com/terms/f/fundamentalanalysis.asp
8. **CoinMarketCap. (2023).** Crypto Fear and Greed Index / Decrypting market sentiments. https://coinmarketcap.com/community/articles/652d33c94f6b081febf1b4b1/
9. **CoinDesk. (2024).** What Are Crypto OTC Desks And How Do They Work?. https://www.coindesk.com/learn/what-are-crypto-otc-desks-and-how-do-they-work/
10. **Ledger. (2023).** Hardware Wallets. https://www.ledger.com/academy/crypto-hardware-wallet
11. **CoinDesk. (2024).** Stablecoins. https://www.coindesk.com/learn/what-is-a-stablecoin/
12. **Internal Revenue Service. (2024).** Digital Assets. https://www.irs.gov/businesses/small-businesses-self-employed/digital-assets
13. **CoinMarketCap. (2024).** The Key Elements of Tokenomics in Crypto Projects. Retrieved from https://coinmarketcap.com/community/articles/6583d58443ac1c05b9f56eae/
14. **CoinTelegraph. (2024).** Crypto index funds simplify investing but challenge blockchain ethos. Retrieved from https://coinmarketcap.com/community/articles/6583d58443ac1c05b9f56eae
15. **Token Metrics. (2024).** What is a Crypto Index Fund? - Complete Guide for Investors. Retrieved from https://www.tokenmetrics.com/blog/crypto-index-fund
16. **Crypto.com. (2023).** Crypto Index Funds: Everything to Know About Diversifying Crypto Portfolios. Retrieved from https://crypto.com/university/crypto-index-funds-everything-to-know-about-diversifying-crypto-portfolios

17. **Investopedia. (2024).** Capitalization-Weighted Index: Definition, Calculation, Example. Retrieved from https://www.investopedia.com/terms/c/capitalizationweightedindex.asp
18. **CoinTelegraph. (2023).** What is a crypto index fund, and how to invest in it? Retrieved from https://cointelegraph.com/news/what-is-a-crypto-index-fund-and-how-to-invest-in-it
19. **GeeksForGeeks.org. (2023).** What are Crypto Indices? Retrieved from https://www.geeksforgeeks.org/what-are-crypto-indices/
20. **Investopedia. (2024).** Artificial Intelligence (AI) in Investing. Retrieved from https://www.investopedia.com/how-to-use-artificial-intelligence-in-your-investing-7973810
21. **CoinDesk. (2023).** Why the Biggest Emerging Markets Are Turning to Crypto. Retrieved from https://www.coindesk.com/consensus-magazine/2023/05/22/why-the-biggest-emerging-markets-are-turning-to-crypto/
22. **Catalini, C., & Gans, J. S. (2016).** Some Simple Economics of the Blockchain. SSRN Electronic Journal. https://papers.ssrn.com/sol3/papers.cfm?abstract_id=2874598
23. **Antonopoulos, A. M. (2014).** Mastering Bitcoin: Unlocking Digital Cryptocurrencies. O'Reilly Media.
24. **Swan, M. (2015).** Blockchain: Blueprint for a New Economy. O'Reilly Media.
25. **Tapscott, D., & Tapscott, A. (2016).** Blockchain Revolution: How the Technology Behind Bitcoin Is Changing Money, Business, and the World.
26. **Ulam Labs (2024).** Understanding Bitcoin ETFs: Risks and Opportunities. https://www.ulam.io/blog/understanding-bitcoin-etfs-risks-and-opportunities
27. **De Filippi, P., & Loveluck, B. (2016).** The Invisible Politics of Bitcoin: Governance Crisis of a Decentralised Infrastructure. Internet Policy Review, 5(3). https://doi.org/10.14763/2016.3.427
28. **Alevtina Dubovitskaya, & Zhigang Xu (2017).** How Blockchain Could Empower eHealth: An Application for Radiation Oncology. https://www.researchgate.net/publication/319428848_How_Blockchain_Could_Empower_eHealth_An_Application_for_Radiation_Oncology
29. **Chohan, U. W. (2022).** Cryptocurrencies: A Brief Thematic Review. SSRN Electronic Journal. https://doi.org/10.2139/ssrn.3024330
30. **Macey, J., & O'Hara, M. (2005).** From Markets to Venues: Securities Regulation in an Evolving World. Yale Law School.
31. **Ankit Gupta (2022).** How to Manage Cryptocurrencies during a Global Crisis: 7 Tips to Look For. https://medium.com/buyucoin-talks/how-to-manage-cryptocurrencies-during-a-global-crisis-7-tips-to-look-for-7029209928b5
32. **Gandal, N., & Halaburda, H. (2016).** Can We Predict the Winner in a Market with Network Effects? Competition in Cryptocurrency Market. https://doi.org/10.3390/g7030016

33. **IRS. (2021).** Frequently Asked Questions on Virtual Currency Transactions. https://www.irs.gov/individuals/international-taxpayers/frequently-asked-questions-on-virtual-currency-transactions

34. **E. George (2023).** DAOs: The New Wave in Organizational Structure. https://www.linkedin.com/pulse/daos-new-wave-organizational-structure-elsa-george-acca/

35. **Nasdaq (2024).** CoinDesk: China Never Completely Banned Crypto. https://www.nasdaq.com/articles/china-never-completely-banned-crypto

36. **Crypto.com (2024).** How to Short Bitcoin (BTC) and Other Cryptocurrencies. https://crypto.com/bitcoin/how-to-short-bitcoin

37. **Investopedia (2024).** 7 Ways to Short Bitcoin. https://www.investopedia.com/news/short-bitcoin/

38. **CoinTelegraph (2024).** How to short Bitcoin on Binance and Coinbase. https://cointelegraph.com/news/short-bitcoin-on-binance-and-coinbase

39. **Wikipedia (2024).** GameStop short squeeze. https://en.wikipedia.org/wiki/GameStop_short_squeeze

40. **Biais, B., Bisiere, C., Bouvard, M., & Casamatta, C. (2019).** The Blockchain Folk Theorem. The Review of Financial Studies, 32(5), 1662-1715. https://doi.org/10.1093/rfs/hhy095

41. **Cong, L. W., & He, Z. (2019).** Blockchain Disruption and Smart Contracts. The Review of Financial Studies, 32(5), 1754-1797. https://doi.org/10.1093/rfs/hhz007

42. **Fisch, C. (2019).** Initial Coin Offerings (ICOs) to Finance New Ventures. Journal of Business Venturing, 34(1), 1-22. https://doi.org/10.1016/j.jbusvent.2018.09.007

43. **Howell, S. T., Niessner, M., & Yermack, D. (2020).** Initial Coin Offerings: Financing Growth with Cryptocurrency Token Sales. The Review of Financial Studies, 33(9), 3925-3974. https://doi.org/10.1093/rfs/hhz131

44. **Schilling, L., & Uhlig, H. (2019).** Some Simple Bitcoin Economics. Journal of Monetary Economics, 106, 16-26. https://doi.org/10.1016/j.jmoneco.2019.07.002

45. **Sockin, M., & Xiong, W. (2020).** A Model of Cryptocurrencies. NBER Working Paper No. 26816. https://www.nber.org/papers/w26816

46. **Zetzsche, D. A., Arner, D. W., & Buckley, R. P. (2018).** Regulating a Revolution: From Regulatory Sandboxes to Smart Regulation. Fordham Journal of Corporate & Financial Law, 23(1), 31-103. https://ir.lawnet.fordham.edu/jcfl/vol23/iss1/2/

47. **Adhami, S., Giudici, G., & Martinazzi, S. (2018).** Why do businesses go crypto? An empirical analysis of initial coin offerings. Journal of Economics and Business, 100, 64-75. https://doi.org/10.1016/j.jeconbus.2018.04.001

48. **Chiu, J., & Koeppl, T. V. (2019).** The Economics of Cryptocurrencies – Bitcoin and Beyond. Bank of Canada Staff Working Paper 2019-40. https://www.bankofcanada.ca/2019/09/staff-working-paper-2019-40/

49. **OECD. (2022)**. The Tokenisation of Assets and Potential Implications for Financial Markets. https://www.oecd.org/en/publications/the-tokenisation-of-assets-and-potential-implications-for-financial-markets_83493d34-en.html

50. **Investopedia. (2024**). Cryptocurrency Wallet: What It Is, How It Works, Types, and Security. https://www.investopedia.com/terms/b/bitcoin-wallet.asp

51. **SEC. (2017)**. Investor Bulletin: Initial Coin Offerings. https://www.sec.gov/oiea/investor-alerts-and-bulletins/ib_coinofferings

52. **Ethereum.org. (2023)**. What is Ethereum? https://ethereum.org/en/what-is-ethereum/

53. **Blockchain Council. (2022)**. DeFi vs. CeFi: Understanding the Differences Between Centralized and Decentralized Finance. https://www.blockchain-council.org/defi/centralized-and-decentralized-finance/

54. **World Economic Forum. (2022)**. Decentralized Autonomous Organizations: Beyond the Hype. https://www.weforum.org/publications/decentralized-autonomous-organizations-beyond-the-hype/

55. **World Economic Forum. (2023**). Decentralized autonomous organizations explained. https://www.weforum.org/agenda/2023/01/everything-you-need-to-know-daos/

www.ingramcontent.com/pod-product-compliance
Lightning Source LLC
Chambersburg PA
CBHW061216220326
41599CB00025B/4654